ROUTLEDGE LIBRARY EDITIONS:
SOVIET SOCIETY

Volume 24

I0093881

THE SOVIET WAY OF LIFE

THE SOVIET WAY OF LIFE

An Examination

MAURICE LOVELL

Routledge
Taylor & Francis Group

LONDON AND NEW YORK

First published in 1948 by Methuen & Co. Ltd.

This edition first published in 2025
by Routledge
4 Park Square, Milton Park, Abingdon, Oxon OX14 4RN

and by Routledge
605 Third Avenue, New York, NY 10158

Routledge is an imprint of the Taylor & Francis Group, an informa business

© 1948

British Library Cataloguing in Publication Data
A catalogue record for this book is available from the British Library

ISBN: 978-1-032-86028-2 (Set)
ISBN: 978-1-032-86430-3 (Volume 24) (hbk)
ISBN: 978-1-032-86437-2 (Volume 24) (pbk)
ISBN: 978-1-003-52752-7 (Volume 24) (ebk)

DOI: 10.4324/9781003527527

Publisher's Note
The publisher has gone to great lengths to ensure the quality of this reprint but points out that some imperfections in the original copies may be apparent.

Disclaimer
The publisher has made every effort to trace copyright holders and would welcome correspondence from those they have been unable to trace.

HOME STUDY BOOKS
General Editor: B. Ifor Evans

THE SOVIET WAY OF LIFE

AN EXAMINATION

by

MAURICE LOVELL

METHUEN & CO. LTD., LONDON
36 Essex Street, Strand, W.C.2

First published in 1948

CATALOGUE NO. 4449/U

THIS BOOK IS PRODUCED IN
COMPLETE CONFORMITY WITH THE
AUTHORIZED ECONOMY STANDARDS

PRINTED IN GREAT BRITAIN

CONTENTS

SCHEME OF ANALYSIS

I. FRAMEWORK

II. ADMINISTRATION

CONTENTS

PART I FRAMEWORK

CHAPTER I
THE ELEMENTS

IN older days it used to be said, 'There is always something new out of Africa'. Historically it would probably be truer to say, 'There is always something new out of Asia'. The migrations of people have normally begun in the East. The most modern instance of novelty from the East has been the flow of information coming into the West from Russia and her allied territories during the past thirty years. A new movement within the experience of man has occurred, and as a result all trifles concerning it, all scraps of intelligence, all the sheaves of non-consecutive figures which it has produced, have been gathered, sometimes painstakingly, often at random, into several libraries-full of books.

Most of these descriptions have expressed a judgment, an attitude, for or against the Soviet way of life. Most of these books have been written by men who have had little understanding of the Russians as a people. They have been concerned to fasten down within an opinion the present mode of organization within the Soviet Union. As a result some have praised as indigenous to the country ways which were essentially foreign or imported; while others have attacked as loathsome products of Socialism, aspects of life which are proper to or automatic in a Euro-Asiatic society. On the other hand there have been some writers who, by origin

I

or training, understood and took for granted the
peculiarities of the country and peoples they were
describing. Painting within the walls of their own
minds they have usually failed to convey a real and
comprehensible picture to the average person in the
world outside the Soviet boundaries.

Apart from the Soviet encyclopaedia, the most
detailed statement concerning the Soviet Union is
that which was written eleven years ago by Sidney
and Beatrice Webb, *Soviet Communism: a New
Civilization?* In its magnificent detail this book took
full account of the 'backwardness' of some of the
peoples who were applying the Soviet experiment,
but as its title hints, it has an ideological basis and
gives the impression of having been written by
intelligent Fabians for Fabians. In another direction, at least three other writers have produced
books of serious content—but on a basis of judgment,
namely, Leonard Hubbard, with his works on Soviet
labour and agriculture; Professor S. N. Prokopovicz,
with his statistical analysis in *Russlands Volkwirt-
schaft unter den Soviets*, and W. H. Chamberlin with
his critical, documented series. Then, among those
who have written with a basic awareness of the
Russian life upon which they were commenting, are
Borodin, Suvarin, Barmin, and Walter Kolarz.
These writers have meant to explain the Soviet
Union—and they are, I suggest, far more comprehensible for the average person outside the Soviet
Union than those writers of the 'Smenavekh school'
who, as Russians in exile, realized even in the early
twenties that Russia, on becoming Sovietized, had
not ceased to be Russia. In mentioning all these
authors I am not endeavouring to estimate the value

of their work, but simply to point out that they had either an ideological basis or were expressing a judgment. Only of the late Sir John Maynard, author of *Russia in Flux* and *The Russian Peasant*, would it not be true to say this; but he did not include in his works a separate detailed statement of the Soviet way of life.

To set down the truth for its own sake, about the Soviet Union, and not to attempt a judgment is more difficult than to pass a mirror without glancing in it. Perhaps the hardest task for humanity is to state the truth simply. It is its success in this task which gives a limpid quality to the New Testament. One reason why it is so difficult to state the truth simply, so far as the Soviet Union is concerned, is that there are so many elements to fuse.

In the first place, it is necessary to emphasize as one element that the Soviet way of life is simply Russian life in a Socialist setting. It is a life lived by Russians; beginning with a Russian manner of swaddling children and ending with a Russian manner of following the uncovered coffin in the hearse. To describe what the Revolution meant and the development of a Socialist way of life in Russia, shall one quote Gogol's famous passage on the flight of the Russian troika, at last speeding at a gallop across the centuries? Shall one explain the underlying pride and the conviction of immense potential force which lay behind Gogol's words? Or shall one rather describe the Russian peasant boy setting out in winter from the collective-farm to join the Red Army? It would be necessary to explain how the family follows him to the end of the village, how the girls watch him pass and how his departure is sealed

with the traditional treble kiss from his father and
mother. But how could one explain that the two
ideas, the launching of the troika and the young
man's departure for the Red Army are two aspects
of the same thing? To attempt to do so would
demand a long book—and all that finally it would
say, is that Russia is the basis of the Soviet way of
life. To understand that way of life it is necessary
first to try to understand Russia; her history, her
disappointments, the previous influences upon her,
the effects on her people of generations of seasonal
labour on the farms. Behind the Supreme Soviet
stands not only Lenin, but also the chattering, well-
meaning, useless Oblomov; and also the energetic,
liberal, powerless minority of the Narodniki.
Oblomov, the symbol of the frustration of the
intellect in nineteenth-century Russia, is a character
in a novel produced by a Russian about Russians.
The Narodniki were Russians of the nineteenth
century who failed to secure the liberation of the
intellect because of the material circumstances of
the Russia around them.

Secondly, because the Soviet way of life is one
application of Socialism, it is necessary to try to
understand the various lines of development of
European Socialist theory and their links with
Russia. The English line of development begins
where you please, with John Ball or Gerard Win-
stanley, or with Robert Owen: to move on through
William Morris, and the Fabians, to Bernard Shaw
and John Strachey. Of its very nature it is a progressive school, in which words and gestures are the
substitute for grenades and revolution. The French
line has never resolved this problem of words or

action. It proceeds through Fourrier, Lammenais, and Proudon on to Sorel, the man of action, Jaurès, the European progressive, and Léon Blum, surest when under trial by the men of Pétain at Riom. The French line is as intellectual as the English is pragmatic. In a country where men are assumed to be equal, the Socialist propagandist has always to build an intellectual edifice above that basis and shout his creed from the pinnacle. Neither of these lines is, by nature, especially satisfying to the Russian thinker. That is not to say that English and French Socialist ideas and writings did not penetrate into Russia in the nineteenth century. But perhaps because Germany was physically nearer, perhaps because of their massive dogmatism, the major German Socialist writers were those who chiefly influenced the leaders of Russian revolutionary thought. The genealogy of the Soviet way of life is given in the text-books as Marx–Engels–Lenin–Stalin.

What the disaffected progressive Europeans found in England was not their theory but a physical refuge. London was at one time or another an asylum for most of them from Herzen to Marx and Lenin. While the British protest movements were passing from one success to another in the Trade Union Acts, the Factory Acts, and the Education bills, Continental Socialism was struggling against a background of the failure of the revolutionary movements of 1848 and of the later Paris Commune.

Meanwhile Russian progressive thought, from the time of Belinski in the 'forties onward, was commenting upon a picture of agricultural serfdom followed after 1861 by agricultural poverty—the

whole within a framework of Tsarist autocracy. All
the currents of contemporary Continental thought
were reflected in the Russia of the nineteenth century
but they were never so powerful as the local circumstances. Russia remained apart and her problems
were her own; even the infiltrations of Continental
thought served more to exacerbate the frustrations
of Russian thinkers than to solve their problems.
Sir John Maynard quotes Donald Mackenzie
Wallace, writing in the seventies of the last century,
as telling us that Russia has accomplished and could
accomplish again political and social evolutions of
a dangerous kind, provided the autocratic power is
preserved and the people remain politically passive.

Referring to the mood of disappointment which
closed in upon Russia after the emancipation from
serfdom of a majority of the population, in 1861,
Sir John Maynard adds: 'The defects of the great
emancipation, after the first flush of disappointment
over the land redemption dues was over, were not
immediately apparent to the mass of the peasantry.
It was otherwise with the eager radical publicists
who had watched the progress of the scheme. They
could not forgive the disappointment of hopes which
had been pitched so high: and a passion of sympathy
with the peasant drove them out into the countryside and fostered the growth of a bitter revolutionary
conviction.'

As the turn of the century neared, all the shades
of political thought generally current in the world
had been pushed to extremes in Russia—by the
local circumstances of a semi-developed country of
poor communications.

What was liberalism in the West was even more

enlightened in Russia; what was traditionalism in Britain was even more obdurately immobile in Russia; what in the West was anarchism or syndicalism was complemented in Russia by Nihilism. The first attempt to supplant by direct action the interminable tentative gropings towards a new form of society occurred in 1905. The very swiftness of the outbreak bears witness to the long ingrowing dissatisfaction which had preceded it—and the outbreak failed. As an element in the understanding of the Soviet way of life, it is necessary to appreciate the extent of the failure of the 1905 insurrection. And beyond this it is necessary to place the 1917 revolution in the context of Russian and Asiatic history.

Russia had no Renaissance. When Wyatt and Surrey were bringing back to England the Italian sonnet, the old city of Kazan near the Volga was disputed between the Russians and the Tartars. For a couple of centuries the Muscovites had either to withstand the horsemen out of Asia or perish. Not till the early eighteenth century did Peter the Great build his city on the Neva, and Tsar Paul died miserably at the hands of a palace clique at a time when the French mob was to see Louis XVI executed for a social idea. Thus when the 1917 revolution occurred and was stabilized in the succeeding years, it came as a break not only with tradition, but also with centuries of failures that were nearly successes and gains that were not consolidated. It led to a loosing of energies not among a people of a few millions but among a nation which had already grown to nearly 150 millions.

But in considering the new course of life of these

millions, it is essential to appreciate the actual, real difficulties encountered in applying Socialism in Russia. In 1919, the industrial proletariat of Russia was still a small and largely undeveloped working-class. Only in a few centres such as the arms factories of St. Petersburg and Tula, the textile works of Tver (Kalinin), the mines of Hughesevka (Stalino), and Kishtim, were there any large numbers of workers with a long-standing inherited skill. Illiteracy of the great majority of peasants meant that it was difficult to convey to them in detail, other than by demonstration, exactly what the new society demanded of them. They could neither appreciate immediately what they were required to do, nor acquire technical skills except over a period of years. An industrial revolution and the colonizing of a continent, for such is Siberia, had to coincide with the application of a new order for the community.

The sheer material difficulties of carrying through this programme were such that the authorities were obliged to think and plan on two lines at once: how to achieve development, and how to maintain themselves at the head of an actually working concern. Consequently certain acts of the Government have been designed as progressive acts in the development of a higher level of civilization; others have been confessedly acts of strategy aimed at strengthening the position of the ruling party and its individuals applying the given programme.

Into any attempt to describe objectively the Soviet way of life must also enter a number of other elements. For example, with the passage of time after 1917, a loss of revolutionary impetus was inevitable. It is one thing to admit such a fact, but quite another thing to assess exactly what of the impetus has been lost. Similarly, with the passage of time new vested interests are an inevitable phenomenon even if they are those of professions and organizations and no longer those of exploitatory classes. Here again the difficulty is not the admission of the fact, but how to describe and what importance to attach to the rise of such professions as the factory director or such organizations as the Film Ministry or such institutions as Narkom-vneshtorg (Commissariat of Foreign Trade). A further element which it is easy to recognize but difficult to explain is the imposed factor of the international responsibilities automatically devolving upon a State which has proved itself a great power. Such responsibilities necessarily have their effects upon the internal life of the community, e.g. the degree of smartness and 'side' in its armed forces, the numbers and standard of skill of its representatives abroad.

The Soviet way of life is compacted of these elements I have mentioned, and many others. Like any way of life it can be fully appreciated only in its own setting. And its setting ranges from the western marshlands of the Polessye to the black coast of Petropavlovsk, from the trappers' hut in the Yakutsk forests to the Admiralty Arch of Leningrad. Since he cannot take the reader with him into this setting, the writer of any book concerning the Soviet system should start with a genuine appreciation that he is describing a world of human beings, and not a macrocosm of applied ideas. He should try to convey the reality that among this group of peoples living the Soviet life there exists somewhere the descendant of the woman who gave birth to Timiryazev, and somewhere a descendant of the woman who gave birth to Genghis Khan. Many wrong judgments spring from regarding this Soviet Union as an entirely schematic world. The lesson that it is a community of erring, sinful, and unequal human beings is perhaps the principal lesson taught by Stalin himself to his party —a lesson which some of the theoretical Older Bolsheviks were unable to learn and for which they perished. But they were actually concerned with and caught up in the experiment of the life which is being tried in Russia. Those who are outside should find it easier, looking on, to regard the Soviet Union as a collection of human beings. Like the ways of man in Britain, America, or any other country, life in Russia is an adaptation of human desires to circumstances—a modification of purpose to inescapable needs and finite human powers.

The system of the Soviets appears and is vertical, monolithic. From a huge base of many millions of people living on a continent, it proceeds upward to one tiny, crenelated, red-walled village in the centre of one city. It rises from the convict camp in the 'taiga' to the telephones on Stalin's desk. Through the farm-councils or village-Soviets the route leads upwards by way of Tiflis and Minsk, Murmansk and Kuibyshev, to the newly-painted, red-carpeted hall of the Supreme Soviet within the precincts of the Kremlin, where the arclights beam and the cameras record every detail of the entry and exit of the giants of the Presidium.

But all along the roads of this system, the

individual facts are relative and shifting. They are unstable like radio-active atoms; and like all relationships among human beings in any place at any time. Only the theory of the system tends to be absolutist and to demand acceptance as dogma. It is the likeness of the system to the structure of a Chinese box which might tend to give the impression that the Soviet Union was an ant-world—a hive of units performing prescribed, necessary, and thoroughly laudatory tasks on various levels of society from aphis-milker to the queen. In fact, however, the most apparent truth regarding the system is the variety of contrasts. Freedom of opportunity, for example, is an indisputable aspect of life in the Soviet Union at present. Views may differ concerning the other 'freedoms', but on that of opportunity there can be no doubt.

The students of Moscow and Leningrad Universities are moreover now busily discussing amongst themselves as successive generations of students always do. They are reassessing the meanings of various basic expressions such as 'democracy', 'human personality', 'leadership', on and on into the night. And during the past twenty years many hundreds of thousands of Soviet citizens have changed their level of income, their profession or calling, even the scope of their demands upon life, not once, but a number of times. I have known men who have spent several years wandering to the Far East and back into Central Russia, doing different jobs here and there. They were exceptional but they gave outcrop evidence of a real seam of opportunity. Equally in this world, schematic in theory, and natural in practice, some schools are good schools as such: others, as schools, are not so good. Some of the factories of one type are of a high standard; others in the same group are wasteful and inefficient.

Even large institutions vary. The Lenin Library strikes the Western mind as well run. The canning industry has visibly improved its standards at a greater rate than some others. The Film Ministry, on the other hand, would seem to a Western mind to have shown excessive caution. In short, it is a human world.

There are two principal unreal attitudes which are commonly adopted in describing the Soviet way of life. The first is the idealistic manner, which so often makes the mistake to which I have just referred, of treating the Soviet Union as a schematic world. This is frequently the method of foreign radicals, especially those from America—well-meaning persons of great yearning who, by way of compensation, import to the Soviet life a neatness and cultured exactitude which swears with the sanitary conditions of Kuibyshev's outskirts during the spring thaw just as much as it would with those of Newcastle or Pittsburgh. Quite apart from any question of politics, the Russians themselves have a tendency to take as fact what exists only as a plan, such as, for example, the painting of their dacha. But within their own surroundings they are at the same time not perpetually deceived. However, if the foreigner is uncritical, there exists such a vigorous wealth of planning within the Russian mind and the Russian language as can lead the foreigner to accept an ideal but unreal picture of the Soviet Union.

The second basically unreal approach is the

pseudo-realistic, that of the disillusioned traveller or the former deportee. If you refer to peasants' houses as 'hovels', and if you load your narrative with descriptions of snow and cold, and ignore the fact that the 'hovel' may have electric lighting, which is still almost a Holy Mystery to the indwellers, and that centuries of self-adaptation to winter have taught them to regard the snow with something like affection—you may not depart from the real facts but you will commit many sins of omission. Furthermore, most Russians have an inbred sus-piciousness. It is unreal, however, to describe their resultant initial reserve as the quietness of 'cowed people'.

Stalin was evidently aware of the prevalence of these two unreal attitudes when he said to a distin-guished American visitor early in 1945, 'Please tell the whole truth about us. State what you actually see'. This was perhaps too brief a dictum, but as such no doubt it was a counsel of perfection.

To fulfil such advice would require the time, observation, and method of Montesquieu. The particular State and the 'Esprit des lois' which need to be described, merit the observation of the dis-cerning Frenchman. Where the Webbs were brilliantly concerned with fact-gathering about the system itself a Montesquieu would have etched his picture more deeply. Here is a world such as he was concerned with; a world with a determining geography, a given people, a balance of adminis-trative regulations and their practice. What would also have pleased the great precursor of the Encyclo-pédistes is the expression of purpose in this State which he would so busily and exquisitely have annotated. What is here in practice is the application, however right, however wrong, of a philosophy. For thirty years Lenin, Stalin, and their companions have been carrying out an experiment such as it was not given to any other of the Utopists, the imaginers of new states, to perform. Plato, Aristotle, and St. Augustine built their cities in words, and Machiavelli, Aquinas, Thomas More and their later colleagues had no opportunity to take and refashion a state after their heart's desire.

To an Englishman, I suggest, the completeness of Plato's republic has something appalling; but it remained within the covers of a book. The Soviet experiment has something of the same completeness, but it has occurred within history and with all the ragged ends of history. Full-scale Socialism has been applied in a particular country, Russia, at a particular time in that country's history.

The Soviet citizen living inside the system is aware of the experiment at every turn. He is constantly reminded of it from the moment when the first news bulletin goes out over the loud-speakers in the streets in the morning. It is with him at the moment when he takes off one of the limited numbers of shoe-designs in order to undress for bed. Whether the individual citizen appreciates the scope and nature of the experiment in which he is taking part, depends naturally on his own level of understanding. This may seem a trite statement since all persons are more or less aware of their surroundings. But awareness of one's surroundings does not necessarily mean that one is politically conscious. The Soviet factory girl tends to have the same happy irresponsibility which is found in youths everywhere. If she takes dancing lessons, she does not ask herself whether they come to her by way of a private teacher or a social institute of a Soviet trade union. The Party worker, on the other hand, has all the normal attributes of determination and slight officiousness of the socially minded or the Committee-man of Britain or the United States. In a different way the intellectual, even where he is perfectly attuned to the system and loyally contributing towards its maintenance, can nevertheless frequently stand aside mentally from the machine and view its process with a humorous aloofness.

During thirty years many prejudices have been built up within a large number of Russians, political prejudices concerning the outside world. These have the limiting effects of all prejudice. They tend to produce an *esprit borné*. In trying to examine the Soviet Union, however, one has to put against this the real value of certain emotional constants in humanity including the Russians, such as pleasure in the society of friends, parental affection, patriotism, etc.

I shall therefore within the limits of this book take each major organ or function of the Soviet society in turn and describe its working not so much in its details as a machine, and still less to make a political judgment, but rather as it concerns the human beings who live that way of life. Perhaps it may be useful to set down not all, but a few things simply. I shall not attempt to assess whether the Soviet way of life has in it promise of those elements of righteousness for which the thinkers, political and moral, of the last centuries have been striving since the discovery of the global world and the earlier break-up of the uniform Christian Church. Within the non-Soviet world this last is the only important question, the task to which, in their different ways, men such as Bishop Gore, Nikolai Berdyaev, Maritain, and General Smuts, have made their contribution. Only in the light of that question would, in my opinion, a judgment concerning the Soviet Union have any value.

It is possible simply to make a descriptive examination of the Calvin experiment in building a new form of society at Geneva. One could also estimate to what extent that particular historic experiment may have approached the Civitas Dei, the city of God. On the same analogy, this book will be merely a description.

CHAPTER II
THE CONSTITUTION

SINCE 1936, the Soviet Union has worked according to the fundamental laws of the Stalin Constitution. This is a detailed instrument of 146 articles and 2 appendices, as a result of various amendments which have been approved from time to time by the Supreme Soviet of the U.S.S.R. The fundamental law is supplemented by written penal and civil codes.

Perhaps because a firmly established Constitution had been many times contemplated by the Romanov dynasty but never pursued, a fully written Constitution was aimed at by the Soviet leaders from the moment of their assumption of power. By 1924 they possessed one covering the entire Union and that document was valid until superseded by the Stalin Constitution in 1936. A country of such size housing many races may, like the United States, find a written Constitution a necessity. A small country such as Great Britain, which is physically separated from the other members of the Commonwealth, would find a written Constitution a hampering affair since whatever fundamental law is necessary has already been established by custom and precedent and what is not can be safely left to manœuvre.

There were no basic changes in the Soviet order as a result of the 1936 document. In many of its articles it reaffirms the general allocation of power which had been stated in the document of 1924. The structure of Government by Councils (Soviets) of People's Deputies had existed in essence, though with modifications later, in the early days of the revolution itself. At that time Lenin considered whether to establish the Russian Duma or Parliament in a new form, on the lines of a Western democracy. He decided that a system of superimposed Councils with ascending responsibilities was more suited to the Euro-Asiatic society with which he had to cope. The official history of the Communist Party of the Soviet Union, referring to the famous 'April theses' of Lenin after his return to Russia in 1917, states that he 'proposed the transition from a parliamentary republic to a republic of Soviets. This was an important step forward in the theory and practice of Marxism. Hitherto, Marxist theoreticians had regarded the parliamentary republic as the best political form of transition to socialism. Now Lenin proposed to replace the parliamentary republic by a Soviet republic as the most suitable form of political organization of society in the transition from Capitalism to Socialism. In the Theses he stated, "not a parliamentary republic—to return to a parliamentary republic from the Soviets of workers' deputies would be a retrograde step—but a republic of Soviets of workers', agricultural labourers' and peasants' deputies throughout the country, from top to bottom".'

Officially the 1936 Constitution is held to represent a fundamental advance on that of 1924—which was the synthesis of Lenin's organization—in that the new Constitution provided for a 'further democratization' of the system. The decision to change the fundamental law was taken in February 1935, and the new document became law in November 1936.

After it had been drafted, the text was circulated throughout the constituent republics for six months, liable to proposals for amendments, before being established in final form.

If the structure of the State was not greatly altered by the new law, its mode of constitutional operation was nevertheless changed. The official explanation given in the history of the Communist Party of the Soviet Union is as follows: 'The change of Constitution was necessitated by the vast changes that had taken place in the life of the U.S.S.R. since the first Constitution had been adopted in 1924. During this period the relation of class forces within the country had completely changed. A new Socialist industry had been created, the kulaks had been smashed, the collective farm system had triumphed, and the Socialist ownership of the means of production had been established in every branch of national economy as the basis of Soviet society. The victory of Socialism made possible the further democratization of the electoral system and the introduction of universal, equal, and direct suffrage with secret ballot.'

For the ordinary citizen this was undoubtedly a great change in the conception of his place within the system. It is doubtful, however, whether he placed the event firmly in its chronology, as it is difficult for any people to assess its own recent history. The period of the New Economic Policy (N.E.P.), in which a semi-capitalist reconstruction of revolutionary Russia was allowed, had been succeeded in 1928 by the five-year plans, the second of which was proving successful. Simultaneously with the collectivization of agriculture (1929–32), the kulak class of prosperous farmers had been eliminated. By the series of State trials, accompanied by purges of the Party and administrative organs which, in 1935, were still working towards their frenzied climax, the possibility of any organized political opposition to Stalin within the Union had been destroyed. If there were to be elections, they could be elections only of representatives to further the carrying out of an already stable system. Thus it was possible to take the step of allowing direct and secret balloting by all adult citizens other than those expressly deprived of civic rights.

All written constitutions read well. Written aims always do. The Soviet Constitution is no exception. With all such documents whether at the time of Hammurabi or in the European states reborn as a result of the past war, the question is the extent to which they are applied. One needs to ask also to what measure a given clause is operated so as to nullify or to exaggerate the value of a large number of other clauses. In any State with a written fundamental law, this depends on the assessment made by the ultimate authority, of the actual degree of political maturity of the populace. Taking into account the cultural level of many millions of the Soviet peoples involved, one might say that the Soviet Constitution took great risks in this respect. Therefore, the application of the law, as I shall describe it, may give some indication of the rate of speed at which the Constitution has become operative since its introduction at the end of 1936. The war years 1941–5, by compelling the declaration of martial law or locally of various degrees of 'state of siege', did modify the rate of application of the 1936 law. It was significant, however, that the 1946 elections were carried through fairly speedily after the final victory with only slight modifications of the electoral procedure, most of them in a liberal sense, such as the creation of special constituencies for Soviet forces serving abroad.

At the present time, in view of the recrudescence of Russian national consciousness, we need to remember that in fact the Russians form only just over half the population of the Soviet Union. The total percentage who are of Slav origin is of course higher. But for those who control the whole Union, the geographical distribution of the population and the diverse histories of the various races are more important than the arithmetic proportions of the Soviet peoples. In working out a Constitution providing for representative government the leaders of the Communist Party have found it necessary to take into account both factors.

Hence, the Supreme Soviet consists of two chambers, each fulfilling a distinct purpose, although they often sit together. The Soviet of the Union is elected on a basis of one deputy to every 300,000 of the population. The Soviet of Nationalities consists of 25 deputies elected from each of the 16 constituent republics; 11 from each autonomous republic; 5 from each autonomous region, and 1 from each national area. In the result the Slavs are naturally still predominant in the Supreme Soviet. The deputies number altogether about 1,300. Of these nearly a quarter do not belong to the Communist Party.

Under the Constitution the highest authority is the Supreme Soviet; but the Presidium of the

Supreme Soviet, a body of 32 persons, exercises the highest authority when the Supreme Soviet is not sitting. The Constitution has articles which further state the powers of the Council of Ministers, indicating that its functions are executive and administrative rather than legislative. Other articles establish the authority of the Supreme Court, and the relations of the Legislature to the Judicature.

In the Constitution are enumerated those subjects which are reserved, i.e. State matters which are centrally controlled from Moscow and apply to the whole Union. The Constitution also lists those which are regional subjects controlled by the local governments of the republics and regions.

As the Supreme Soviet meets only twice a year normally, and for short periods, as has been the custom in the early history of the representative legislatures of a number of countries, the making of regulations and administration are delegated to a greater extent than is the case in Great Britain or the United States. In fact the Soviet Constitution does provide all the legal safeguards, just as the American Congress and the Supreme Court are provided with safeguards against the unfettered use of the Administration's authority.

In the Soviet Union, however, day-to-day power lies in the hands of the competent. The general populace is meanwhile being coached in the application of authority which never previously in history have they enjoyed. Equally, the Constitution provides for the distinction of the Legislature, Executive, and Judicature. That separation which has arisen as practice in our country—over which our fathers fought three centuries ago at Worcester and

Derby—is set down in writing in the Soviet Constitution. Naturally, however, where a great deal of authority is delegated, and where a system is so new that there exists no large body of case-law as an independent reference, the three functions of Legislature, Executive, and Judicature, tend to shade one into the other. All decrees of the Presidium have to be approved by the Supreme Soviet ,and all acts of the Ministers can be called into account by the Supreme Soviet. In practice, such examination of the Presidium or the Council of Ministers would be *post hoc*; and in the intervals between the sessions of the Supreme Soviet some scores of decrees are issued.

Since the Soviet Union is governed by a system of 'councils of workers' and peasants' representatives', it is necessary to inquire to what extent this is a correct name. By now, it would be far more correct to call the members of the various local or major councils: 'people of working-class or peasant origin'. A certain few are descendants of the former 'bourgeoisie', but as a rule descendants of this class have gone into the professions rather than into political life. The development of Soviet society as a modern whole has, however, created many types —engineers, doctors, scientists, professional politicians, and professional administrators—who themselves are neither workers nor peasants.

The Soviets of earlier revolutionary days have, however, by means of the Constitution, been stabilized into an immense structure. This pyramid of Councils from the 'selsoviet' (village council) to the Presidium, is confusing to read about, and when correlated with the structure of the all-Union and

B

Union-Republic Commissariats and the Party, can
be bewildering. An enthusiastic or pedantic delving
into the mysteries behind the myriads of initials (e.g.
N.K.I.D., Sovtorg, Narkomles, Byurobin, A.S.S.R.),
can lead one nowhere; or to the conclusion that the
system is in fact very simple. The smaller unit is
usually simply a replica of the larger unit. The
system has opportunities of renewing itself by
draughts of water from the spring of the people—
and over the past twenty years the names of persons
in evidence have frequently changed. This fact,
accompanied by a flow of experiments in administration as well as in economics, has made the picture
puzzling to most people abroad. The same would
probably be true of the picture of any continent
housing many nationalities. The Soviet structure,
as such, is no more complex than that of the United
States; and the ordinary citizen's opportunities of
electing those who apply the system both locally
and nationally are about as numerous, though they
may not occur so frequently.

The difference lies in that with the American two-
party system whole administrations change, while
in the Soviet Union final power has, for the past
twenty years, been concentrated in the hands of
roughly the same few men. In addition, the leading
members of the Communist Party are also leading
members of the Presidium and of the Council of
Ministers and of the State Committee of Defence.
Such plurality was probably inevitable in an
immense society which had to start from nought:
with a ruined economy, a ruined administration,
and a people truncated of its ruling elements. To
the onlooker, however, this doubling of functions by

the same people increases his difficulty in understanding how the system works.

In fact, the system ordained by the Constitution is relatively simple, and to an Englishman it would tend to appear theoretically constructed, because the functions of the regional and republican authorities are so clearly defined and follow so closely the pattern of the all-Union authoritative bodies. Thus it lacks that element of the illogical, or of suppleness, which is the distinguishing feature of many of our own institutions, especially those which are basic to our way of life. In itself the structure of the Soviets is not so much involved as multifarious. The pattern is, however, almost the same for the smallest 'rayon' (district) as well as for the largest republic. There are fifteen Soviet Socialist republics and one Federative Soviet Socialist Republic. Within these are a number of autonomous republics usually inhabited by individual nationalities of a more advanced stage of development; some autonomous regions usually inhabited by distinct nationalities who are limited in their numbers or resources, and some national areas inhabited by races who are not so far advanced as automatically to merit an autonomy of their own. Each of the sixteen Constituent republics is divided into 'oblasts' or provinces, and these in turn are divided into 'rayons' or districts. In certain of the republics there are administrative areas or 'krais', which are, roughly speaking, intermediate between republics and oblasts. On each level within this framework of the Union there is an executive committee charged with general administration. This committee operates side by side with the Communist Party Committee of the particular area, and with the local organs of the Government Departments and the State Planning Commission.

This enormous range of committees has to be staffed. To find the necessary administrators for a large country in a short period, even were the system to remain constant, would be a formidable task. To do so when the previous hierarchy has been overthrown and a new one is in process of development, is naturally still more difficult. And if experience in administration has previously been restricted to a small class, all of whom have been eliminated or rendered ineligible for office, then the task must pass beyond the possible. If several posts are held by each of the really competent and if the government is extremely centralized, as Lenin understood, the task may be pulled back within the bounds of the possible—but the strain upon the available administrators will be wearing. Men will be made or broken in such circumstances. To some extent this has been the case of the Soviet Union in the past twenty-five years. Administration is an art and those gifted in this art who remained to the Russia of 1921 were pitiably few.

Despite many changes, a number of the present provinces still coincide with the boundaries of the 'Guberniye' of Tsarist days. But the Governors of the provinces were not held responsible for developing their regions at a breakneck speed. Their duties, it is true, were not only political but also to some extent economic, from the time of Catherine the Great onward. Nevertheless, they were not expected to assist in creating a Utopia. No blame attached to them if they did not take upon themselves the strain of overhauling within a few years the industrial output and technical efficiency of the great Western Powers. But this is precisely what has been expected of the local Soviet administrator. Total planning of the life of the State has meant that not only Moscow or Leningrad but every region of the Soviet Union has to fulfil its part in the building of 'Socialism in our time'. The all-pervading propaganda, the urgency of official slogans, have led some local executive committees from time to time into misguided zeal; especially when they were inexperienced administrators. The oft-quoted instance of such an outbreak of zeal was that of certain committees, especially in central Russia, at the time of the land collectivization of 1929–30. When the domestic pets of some districts had been issued with number-cards, it was time for Stalin to call a halt and to follow this with his famous encyclical 'Dizzy with Success' (*Leninism*: J. V. Stalin, p. 333). This zeal for an immediate revolution in the nature of agriculture led also to much bitterness among the Kuban Cossacks, the Turkmens, and others.

But viewed broadly, these twenty-five years of bewildering change and furious development have proved a highly selective school for administrators. A type of Soviet executive has been produced who would have given pleasure to Peter the Great. That brilliant *énergumène* tried to carve a similar type out of his nobility in a similarly short time. He, too, had some success, but perhaps would have achieved greater results had he widened the basis for his selection in the manner of the Soviet authorities. No one is now barred from office—especially since the sons of the former bourgeoisie have been gradually readmitted into full civic rights, and the older knowledgeable professors have come out of their obscurity.

The principal feature, however, of Soviet administration has been the creation of a new and somewhat un-Russian personality. The man who nowadays bears on his shoulders the problems of a province is both young and old. He is hard-bitten, but because he has been exclusively concerned with work he is in some ways naïve. Alert and enthusiastic, he is also cautious. He spends his youth generously and is prematurely aged. As a foreigner, one does not often meet these senior administrators, but when met, the characteristics of their type are at once obvious. No one could mistake for example the cold, clear mind and immense capacity for work of Alexandr Shcherbakov, General Secretary of the Moscow Communist Party and Head of the Political Department of the Red Army, who died in his prime in 1945. Similarly, no one could fail to note the infectious ability to 'get things done' of Dmitri Papanin, the Head of the Northern Sea Administration; or the bluff shrewdness of Miterev, Commissar of Health. Most of the administrators and of those elected to representative organs by popular vote as a consequence of their past public work, are members of the Communist Party. Sometimes, however, they did not originally graduate in the Party. Some have proved themselves as 'bespartinye bolsheviki' (non-Party Bolsheviks) actively co-operating with the régime, and thus have been advanced in the administration or have been able to secure nomination as candidates in Soviet elections. In local districts, both classes of the elect are probably well known to their people. Since under the Constitution local government officials and other administrators have a right to be elected to the local or central Soviets, the tendency is for a large number of such people to be elected because of their prominence in the public mind. This is perhaps inevitably so in a fully socialized state.

The voter and even those whom he elects locally are, however, a long way from the centre of power. The province of Kursk is almost as distant as Semipalatinsk. No informality of manner among the central administrators helps to bridge this distance. No Soviet legislators sit on the Treasury bench with their feet on the table. With its success the manners of the Union have become formal. Persons of rank in official life are always given their full titles and the higher the rank the more formal the effect. This delight in the honour attached to grade or rank is in keeping of course with the history of Russia and with the spirit of Asia. The little man in the steppe-village is in fact at a great distance from the bell at the gate-tower of the Kremlin which tells the inner guard that another motor-car has been allowed to enter.

It is only fair to mention that the wireless, the press, the news-reels of ceremonies and parades help to keep the little man aware in a modern way that this is his State. The present respect for authority in the Union of Soviets, where rank is not inherited, is of course different from that which is to be observed in the Russian literature of a century ago. Moscow and the Kremlin have their additional awe for the provincial because they are to a greater extent approachable than was the case in the past.

The heartfelt sigh 'V Moskvu, v Moskvu' (To Moscow, to Moscow) of Chekhov's *Three Sisters* echoes
in the emotions of Soviet provincial audiences just
as it did in the theatres of forty years ago—but
with this difference, that even the smallest provincial
may at some time find this wish granted. He may
go simply as a member of a team of gymnasts to
perform before the Government in the Red Square
on 1 May. He or she may also go as an elected
deputy of the Supreme Soviet; and enter the walled
Kremlin in one of the cathedrals of which lie the
bones of Ivan the Dread and the son Ivan whom he
murdered. To the onlooker at a session of the
Supreme Soviet, nothing is more fascinating than
the half-concealed pleasure and the awed solemnity
of the deputies from Tajikistan or the Oirot autonomous province in the heart of Asia. They move
with studied nonchalance in the corridors and halls
of the great building designed by Kazakov and
listen to the lengthiest speeches packed with figures
from a White-Russian Commissar with a silence and
a concentration which must be unique in the world's
legislative assemblies.

But the Supreme Soviet meets normally only
twice a year, and life is lived daily and under a
constant demand for more food, more goods, in the
fishing villages of Kamchatka and the tea planta-
tions of Uzbekistan. The importance therefore of
the Communist Party within this enormous structure—quite apart from its significance as a political
body or as representing a particular philosophy—is
that it forms a bloc, a permanent cement. The
decisions of the supreme authority (in those high
regions of State where legislature and executive are

synonymous) are made known to the subordinate
levels of the Party in good time. By the Party,
public opinion is shaped to meet these decisions
when they take effect. Equally public opinion,
which formulates and coagulates slowly in the
factories and among the collectives, finds its way
upwards through the Party. It would be false to
assume that this opinion is always negative. It is
frequently constructive and even enthusiastic in a
manner which is difficult to understand for those
who do not share the quickness and emphasis of
Slav emotions.

Subject to the amendments which may be proposed by the committee, mainly of party theoreticians, now sitting under the chairmanship of M.
Vishinski, this then is the nature of the Soviet
system of which the fundamental laws are laid down
in the Constitution. The danger for such a large
and preconceived structure, however simple in its
architecture, is that not only its pinnacles but also
its main fabric might get out of touch and alignment
with its foundations in the people. Of this Stalin
showed himself aware in his essay on 'Defects in
Party Work'. 'We may take it as a rule,' said the
far-seeing Georgian, 'that as long as the Bolsheviks
maintain connexion with the broad masses of the
people they will be invincible. And, on the contrary,
as soon as the Bolsheviks sever themselves from the
masses and lose their connexion with them, as soon
as they become covered with bureaucratic rust, they
will lose all their strength and become a mere cipher.'

Whether this advice has been heeded no individual
onlooker could say and only history can show. For
the present we are left with the statements made by

the Soviet leader in his speech before the first
post-war elections, namely:

'The Soviet State system has been victorious—
the multi-national Soviet State has stood up to all
trials.

'In the past the Communists viewed people who
did not belong to the Party with a certain distrust
due to the fact that not infrequently various
bourgeois groups camouflaged themselves under the
banner of non-Party citizens. Times are different
now, and persons are now divided from the bourgeoisie by a barrier which is called the Soviet
structure of society and which unites the non-Party
citizens with the Communists into one common
collective of Soviet people.'

PART II   ADMINISTRATION

CHAPTER III
THE PARTY

THE Soviet system is intended to provide for a class-less society. In the maintenance of that society there are those who do more work of a social character, and those who do less. Those who do more are grouped together in the Communist Party. Within the State, the Party performs a function which, of necessity, distinguishes its members from the normal citizenry. At the time of the Revolution, Party members were in a minority even in the Soviets of workers and peasants who held the factories and seized the land in a spirit of opposition to Tsardom and the existing social order. With the development and stabilization of the Soviet system, the Party has obtained effective control in all branches of the State. It has also become an *élite*. This *élite*, which is spread throughout the Union, exists side by side with and shares part of its power with the *élite* of the administration and of the army. But as the persons forming these last two groups are also often members of the Communist Party, it must be said that in the *ultima ratio* there is only one *élite*. What is often not sufficiently appreciated outside the Union is the number of persons holding high posts in the administration, in industry, and the army, who are not members of the Party.

The distinguishing characteristic of members of

the Party is that they are expected not merely to live within the Soviet system, but actively to aid in the maintenance and development of the system. In such a huge organism as the Soviet Union with an inherited low standard of living which it has not yet succeeded in transforming, and with a wide variety of cultural levels of the masses, there is an immense need of persons prepared to take the initiative in social work.

The range of 'obshchestvennaya rabota' (social work) is so broad that much of it could not be carried out unless there were a hard core of persons capable of undertaking leadership in these matters. Logically it is not necessary that these persons should belong to a particular political party. The social work which is carried out in Russia includes such diverse subjects as the organization and leadership of clubs; leadership of Pioneer and Komsomol groups; organization and leadership of sections of the civilian defence organization 'Osoaviakhim'; organizing and conducting evening classes; the arranging of irregular social activities such as the collection of State loan subscriptions, pre-election meetings, parades, volunteer working parties for clearing the streets of snow, etc. Thus it is clear that this aspect of the life of the community covers much which cannot be fulfilled by the intelligentsia alone. In fact, within the Soviet system, Communists are also needed among the intelligentsia to take the lead in organizing the social life of this branch of the community. In some countries, social work, being unorganized, tends to become the particular responsibility of the intelligentsia (as distinct from intellectuals). In nineteenth-century Russia, this tended to be also the case with the liberal intelligentsia who produced a number of persons of outstanding social conscience and integrity. Indeed, in some directions, particularly among schoolteachers, they established local traditions of service, the influence of which has lingered on in various places even till to-day.

But being in its origins a proletarian organization and a revolutionary group determined on no compromise, the Bolshevik Party of Russia was aloof from the intelligentsia. At the time of the Revolution it accepted aid from individual 'bourgeois intellectuals' with some surprise and in a purely pragmatic manner. It was not until the middle 'thirties that Stalin decided that a new intelligentsia had arisen whom it was possible to acknowledge as a separate element within the State. Since then all Soviet decrees, writings, and speeches have recognized that the nation consists of workers, peasants, and intelligentsia. This recognition was possible because by that time there were Communists among all three classes. During the war this process of the acceptance of the intelligentsia was taken a stage farther. All sections of the community were expected to make their special contribution to the war effort. The intelligentsia was encouraged to make its contribution in its own way. Poets went to the front in uniform—to recite and to write poetry. Leading descriptive writers became war correspondents. Honoured Artists of Tajikistan danced on lorry platforms to entertain the troops.

The war brought a further broadening of the attitude of the Party towards persons of individual capacity and initiative. What occurred was that, as large numbers of outstanding fighters and others prepared to take military initiative emerged, they were often invited to join the Party with little or no preparation in a political sense. This election of persons who had distinguished themselves in war rather than politics, was more rapid than the Party had normally allowed. For the Party has always been a small minority within the State. There were some 46,000 members only, at the beginning of 1917. Although the Party increased to a quarter of a million a year later, the tendency has always been to restrict numbers and furthermore to haul them down rapidly from time to time. Similarly, membership has been allowed to increase speedily on occasions, for particular purposes. Thus, in the latter part of 1921, the Party was thoroughly purged and reduced from about three-quarters of a million to half a million. In 1924, after the death of Lenin, the membership was recruited up to 800,000. From that date the numbers rose steadily to 1,700,000 in 1930. With industrialization and collectivization going on concurrently, membership was brought up to 2·5 million by 1932. The composition of the Party in 1930 was: industrial workers, 65·3 per cent; peasants, 20·2 per cent; brain workers 13·4 per cent; unclassified, 1·1 per cent.

Power lies with the Party, and it is significant that in 1930, although the membership was spread over all nationalities within the Union, Russians and Ukrainians formed two-thirds of the members. This is simply a physical confirmation of the fact that the Communist Party is the Party of Russia. In its collective mentality it reflects the good and the bad qualities of the Russians, of their ways of thought, their absolutisms, their emotional wish to please,

their communal determination to punish the individual who has set himself apart. At the same time
it expresses the yearning of the Russian to discipline
himself, a yearning largely arising out of failures in
his past history. In some ways it acts within the
State as the conscience of Tolstoi acted within that
ageing genius, spurring him and causing him to
criticize even his greatest successes.

To this extent at least the writers of the 'Smenavekh' group were correct. They held that the
Revolution was merely a turning-point in the history
of Russia. What they did not sufficiently recognize
was that the Bolshevik Party, which had sent them
into exile, was itself a Russian party and as such
would not miraculously disappear when once the
traditional characteristics of Russia had emerged
from the dust of the revolutionary era.

The fact that this is a Russian party helps at least
to explain what an Englishman would regard as its
'fanaticism', its demands for complete subjection of
the individual member to its collective will. Lenin
and later Soviet writers, such as Yaroslavski, have
attacked any attempt to describe this fanaticism
as religious. But if the demand of the Party
was not for the surrender of the individual soul, it
was at least a demand for the unquestioned use of
the individual personality. It is probably necessary
to examine this mentality of the Party on the spot
and to absorb its atmosphere before it becomes
possible for an outsider to understand the purge
period with its seemingly incomprehensible State
trials and confessions. On the spot it is also possible
to understand the mentality which demands that
'the Party must always be right'.

For the Old Bolsheviks, the way to an improvement in human life lay through the Party and its
cause. I think that it must be admitted as a fact
that for many of them there appeared to be no
other way. Within the Party they could argue
policy. They could struggle for their own policy
within the Party. Kamenev and Zinovyev, for
example, twice recanted lines of policy which the
Party under Stalin held to be heretical, rather than
accept severance from the Party. Consequently
when the Party turned upon many of the Old
Bolsheviks, they went through a period of mental
crisis which was not simply the product of the law
and the process of the trials. Their confessions, I
suggest, were in varying degrees explanations or
expiations towards the Party rather than to the
judges.

The period of mounting grimness from 1934 to
1938, culminating in the Yezhov purge, is now past.
Its peculiar atmosphere has faded. What has not
ended is the constant and vigorous assertion throughout all the organs of government and of opinion that
the Party line at any given moment is the correct
one. The change of the Party through the years
from a revolutionary organization to the 'leaven' of
an existing society, has not altered the absolutism
of the Party's character. However, the members of
the Party change with the years and consequently
the Party will change. The members of to-day have
new skills, new modes of life, and new standards
which they have come to accept as needs rather
than as aspirations.

The qualifications for membership are searching.
Integrity *vis-à-vis* the Soviet State is essential.

Willingness to undertake responsibility or at least to 'get things done' is a second demand. A probationary period of some two or three years as a 'Candidate' was required before the war, and although a person who was previously a member of the Komsomol (All-Union Leninist Communist Union of Youth) could obtain an easier entry, this was not automatic.

Membership, although it confers privileges, is not a sinecure. The individual member is expected to take part in educational work of one kind or other, and in the organization of all aspects of 'Socialist emulation'. He can expect to be moved from one post to another with less security of tenure than, for example, that of an ordinary skilled worker. Conversely, he may be retained in a post where the Party considers that he is most needed, while other skilled workers amongst his colleagues might choose to move to another factory or institution. The energetic Party member frequently has little time for home life owing to his social activities. And in recent years he has been increasingly expected to maintain high standards of morality, sobriety, and intelligence. Scandal might bring him into disgrace; drunkenness in public could easily wreck his career.

Many Russians regard such an existence as 'a dog's life'. At the same time, Party membership confers a certain authority and greater opportunities of acquiring material advantages such as flats, jobs, travel facilities, and equipment of all kinds. This does not mean that all Party workers live a life of greater material comfort than the average citizen. It appears that many do not avail themselves of all the facilities which could lie open to them because

of their position. But with the growth of the
'permanence' of the Soviet Union, Party membership has tended to become the means of entry to a
career. One Party member explained to me frankly:
'Of course, there are many careerists. I suppose that
is unavoidable. And if they do the work, it may not
matter so much.' Another aspect of the gradual
consolidation of the Party position, is that the
fervent Leninism of the Old Bolsheviks has tended
to be replaced by efficient compliance with the
existing rules of an established society—or by a
more positive, striving practicality which can be
roughly described as 'Stalinist technique'.

The Party has, with the passing of time, developed
its own fashions and its own modes of address. A
small instance of this is the use of the word 'comrade'
between Party members. Members of the general
public refer to each other as 'citizens'. The Party
member can usually be recognized in a group either
by his clothing or his manner. He is vaguely
reminiscent of a French business man, often complete
as to *portefeuille*. In manner he is formal, correct,
and sometimes alternates a curious punctillio with
a deliberate familiarity or 'proletarian' approach.
These external characteristics and especially the
Party mode of speech are not the same as those of
the intellectuals. The intelligentsia (comprising, but
of course reaching far beyond, the intellectuals) has
invented its own jargon, and has its own witticisms
in its clubs. They are modern witticisms, topical,
rarely lasting. The Party member in his speech
disposes more often of the ruling slogans of the
period. That is part of his function and in a sense
its penalty.

The reputation of the Party is maintained by a persistent, all-embracing output of propaganda. The Party worker is made an example, and the qualities which he should possess are exalted in the Press and on the screen. This exhortation forms part of the total system of Soviet internal propaganda which will be described later. That of the Party has all the aspects of a cult. There are cult sections of book shops, and even special shops in which Party literature, slogans, plaster busts, and drawings of the principal Party figures of the past and present can be obtained. Flags and all other equipment for the decking out of Pioneer, Komsomol, and Party buildings can be purchased. It might be said that such trappings are reminiscent of the Nazi party, but equally they may remind one of some of the well-known religious art and book shops of London or Paris or of Boy Scout shops in various parts of the world. The cult aspect of the Party comes to the fore in the schools, among the Pioneers and the Komsomol youth. Nowadays it is perhaps the social responsibilities of the Party which are most emphasized in the schools—side by side with instruction in the working of the Soviet system. The Pokrovski and Buryakov schools of history, which, in a greater or lesser degree, interpreted history in terms of 'class struggle', have been abandoned. Their influence has died from the text-books. As a corollary, the position of the Party as an 'instrument of class struggle' is no longer stressed as it was. The young Pioneers whose organization comprises children between the ages of seven and fifteen, are not taught to become class fighters but Soviet citizens. The organization is closely linked with the Party and the members receive elementary instruction in Party theory, but their main activities are recreational. In many of its activities it resembles the Scout movement as it also does in its dress. Far more time is spent in organized games and excursions and in acquiring road sense, etc., than in absorbing theory. Among the Komsomol, greater attention is paid to Party instruction. Grouping young people between the ages of fifteen and twenty-five, it is the forcing-bed of the Party. Since it consists of young people—though some of its leaders are in their thirties—the Komsomol organization is more idealistic than mechanistic. Its tenor is serious. Among Soviet youth, and even among the university students, there are many whom its earnestness does not attract; just as there are many youths in Western countries who prefer dance or cycling clubs to Church youth societies. Those whom it does attract usually have, by nature, a liking for social work or what we in this country should recognize as 'an elder brother complex'. Altogether, the State's capital investment in the Komsomol organization is heavy. The attractions which it can offer to its members in the way of excursions, camping, and shooting clubs, gymnasiums, etc., are considerable.

Those persons who have been 'candidates', and graduated to full Party membership, are obliged to attend frequent Party meetings and lectures at which the latest programmes, slogans, etc., are explained to them. Within the security of these meetings there is considerable discussion. The Russian has not and presumably never will abandon discussion or the vigorous expression of his own ideas. Gogol, Dostoevski, Tolstoi, Chekhov, have drawn the picture of the articulate and often eloquent Russian. The material remains the same to-day even if cast in a new mould, the product of which is intended to be useful rather than amusing or decorative.

Lastly, the cult aspect of the Party is demonstrated by 'agitpunkty' throughout the Union. These local centres of Party propaganda activity resemble a mixture of a citizens' advice bureau and a British political party committee-room. Many are situated at railway stations where they also provide sustenance for the travelling Party member. During the war these were often useful as soup kitchens. Normally, however, they provide Party literature for Party members, such as 'Sputnik Agitatora' and 'Bloknot Agitatora', or answer questions from the general public on Party points.

If in a community of 190 millions only some 6 millions belong to the single Party, it is obviously true to say that 'the ordinary citizen' is not a member. This is doubly true in Russia. Firstly, those who have joined the Party have done so for a purpose and may therefore be considered to have distinguished themselves from the remainder of the citizenry. Secondly, the probationary period, which before the war lasted at least two years but often longer, is a formative, educational phase.

Naturally it is also true that the members of the Party come from the people. But 'proletarian origin' is in itself no longer a qualification for membership, i.e. to be a worker and to profess the beliefs of the Party will not be sufficient as qualifications for membership. Nowadays it is also necessary to be a proved organizer or social worker among the ranks

of industry or of the army or one of the learned
professions. The Party has for some become a profession in itself—but the general demand made upon
the Party member in recent years, especially during
the war, has been that he should set a practical
example to his fellows rather than be able to exhort
them with the most orthodox theory.

This demand on the Party member that he should
set an example is of course not new. Omelets are
not new, but there are several ways of making them.
The general relationship between the Party and the
State and the Trade Unions had been laid down by
Stalin as long ago as 1927 when a delegation of
American workpeople visited the Soviet Union for
the first time. Stalin then said in the deliberate,
point-by-point style, which is characteristic of him:

'What shape does this guidance take, this control
of the Government of the U.S.S.R. by the workers'
party, the Communist Party?

'Firstly, the Party endeavours to have its best
and most active fighters . . . placed in all the responsible posts in the Government. It does this through
the Soviets and Congresses, and is generally successful because the workers and peasants trust the
Party.

'Secondly, the Party constantly checks the work
of the administration and of the various officials,
and corrects mistakes and remedies defects. . . . It
assists in enforcing the decisions of the Government
and endeavours to secure the support of the mass
of the people for these measures. No important
decisions are arrived at without consulting the
Party.

'Thirdly, in determining the plans and policies of

any of the departments of government, whether in industry or agriculture, trade or cultural advancement, the Party lays down the general line and formulates instructions regarding the character and direction of the work.'

That was Stalin's clear definition of the control of the Government by the Party. Asked about the position of the Party *vis-à-vis* the Trade Unions, Stalin added:

'The Party cannot give direct instructions to the trade unions, but the Party instructs the Communists who are members of the trade unions. You know that there are Communist groups in the trade unions just as there are in the Soviets, in the co-operatives and elsewhere, and it is their duty by persuasion and argument to convince the unions, Soviets, co-operatives, etc., that they should adopt decisions in harmony with the general policy and instructions of the Party. . . . In this way unity of action is secured without which everything would be turned upside down, and there would be continual interruptions in the work of these proletarian organizations.'

The major difference between then and now is probably as follows. Soviet society has become internally more complicated, and cadres have been created in many professions, of persons whose work and the rewards attached thereto would normally fill their lives. The Party therefore recruits in part from among people who are already on the road to becoming distinguished. This is particularly so in industry and in the army, as well as to some extent among the learned professions. Many such persons make their own profession their career and do not join the Party; but few would persistently refuse if it were suggested to them that they should, since such refusal might easily be regarded as disaffection. It is true, however, that rewards of many kinds and privileges are to be gained otherwise than through membership of the Party. Many Heroes of the Soviet Union, for example, have not been members of the Party at the time of their decoration, although it is in the nature of ruling parties that they should first reward their own members for services and feats performed by them. Similarly there are many industrial workers who have earned the title of Stakhanovite and the rates of pay which go with such distinction—without being members of the Party. Lastly, there is an unorganized number of persons who voluntarily engage in social work of various kinds and yet do not belong to the Party. The general term applied to such people is 'bes-partynye bolsheviki' (non-party bolsheviks). Their existence within the State was admitted by Stalin in the middle 'thirties; and both at the elections of 1937 and 1946 such persons were allowed to present themselves as candidates in the elections for the various Soviets, from All-Union to local district councils.

While much scrutiny would be given to anyone of social purpose who came before the public as a 'Bolshevik' outside the Party, the backing of the Party itself gives an immediate authority to an ordinary member which is not held as of right by the 'bespartynii bolshevik'. This measure of stability and self-assurance lends importance inside the system to the humblest 'partorg' (party organizer). In the era of revolutionary change since 1917, the

'partorg' has been a stabilizing factor in many
places where new life was being created in circumstances of great difficulty. Where new factories
were being built and new settlements constructed
he has been able to aid the ordinary worker, the son
of generations of peasants, to cope with circumstances and gradually to achieve bearable conditions
and establish local rights.

This cycle might be put in other words. The
Party created the Revolution; the Revolution
created necessity, together with achievement; and
necessity has created a role for the Party member.
One cause of his strength which can enable him to
fulfil that role, is that once settled in any given spot
the Party man must join the local 'yacheika' (Party
section)—either that of his industry or of the collective farm or district. Thus he comes in touch with
others who have local power. He is consequently
able to raise on a suitable level many an issue
affecting those citizens with whom he is in personal
contact. The shape of the Party of which he is one
unit, is that of 'democratic centralism'—roughly
corresponding with the Chinese box structure of the
State itself. This has been described in a Soviet
text-book as follows:

'All Party organs are autonomous with regard to
purely local issues, but the organization which has
charge of an entire district is a higher and more
authoritative body than the merely sectional
groups, and has the right to alter, reject, or approve
the decisions of its subordinate organizations.

'Every Party member must join some nucleus and
work with it. These sections (yacheiki) are organized
not on a territorial basis but by industries. Each

Communist is a member of the section in the plant where he is employed. All Communists in any given district or city ward are included in the corresponding district, ward, or regional organization. Authority is embodied in the local general meeting, conference, or central congress, as the case may be. These gatherings elect a committee which is the executive organ and manages current activities.'

Thus the Communist Executive Committee building in any Soviet town or village is the ultimate seat of power in the neighbourhood. Consequently, the Central Executive Committee of the whole Union housed in Moscow is, in many ways, the key to an understanding of the Soviet Union. Within it are fought out whatever fights occur. Trends and tendencies of policy represented by this or that committeeman succeed with his success—decline with him, or fade via the uncomfortable coulisses of the 'kandidaty' away into the oblivion of ordinary membership or even expulsion. 'Kandidaty' are prospective full members of the Committee, and it should be explained that it is possible to be elected from their number into full membership of the Committee and later to lose that place and fall back into the ranks of the candidates. Above the Central Committee sits the almost unchanging Politburo, which takes the principal political decisions of the Party; but the Central Committee has changed considerably in its composition with the years especially as a result of the five-year period of trials and purges.

The press and propaganda section of the Central Committee, headed by Alexandrov, determines and explains official opinion within the Union. This

section is charged with reporting on Party theory
to the leaders of the Party and with interpreting
government decisions to the country in the light of
Party theory. It has as a backing all the resources
of the Marx-Lenin Institute in the centre of Moscow,
which houses a vast collection of political and
historical books and documents. Alexandrov's post
is automatically one of the most important in the
Soviet State: significantly, it was he who wrote the
two lengthy articles published throughout the Union
a short while after the German onslaught on Russia,
explaining that the war which had begun in 1939 as
an imperialist war had become a war of national
liberation. Equally, when in 1942, the group of
foreign correspondents in Moscow invited a number
of prominent Soviet officials to a lunch following the
signature of the Anglo-Soviet pact, it was Alexandrov
who outlined the attitude of the Soviet Union to the
events of the moment and how he would like them
to be regarded by the correspondents. The Central
Committee of the Party also has its links with the
Defence Council and with the higher State security
bodies, these deriving partly from the system of
pluralities of posts among leading members of the
State and partly from the old connexions between
the Party and the All-Russian Extraordinary Commission for the Suppression of Counter-Revolution,
Sabotage, and Speculation (Cheka).

The Politburo works from the Kremlin, holding
its regular weekly meetings, although its members,
numbering only fifteen, have ample opportunities of
seeing each other more frequently, especially in the
late evening. This body is the nearest approach in
the Soviet Union to the British Cabinet. A purely

Party organ, it has not the constitutional status of the Presidium of the Supreme Soviet or the Council of Ministers. On the other hand, all members of the Politburo have many other posts in the State from Generalissimo Stalin to Malenkov, member of the Presidium. It is significant, however, that for many years Stalin needed to be only the First General-Secretary to the Politburo to be able to retain his mastery over the whole system of State. In his struggle with the opposition of Right and Left within the Party, Stalin was in fact sufficiently powerful as to show leniency. Twice he forgave the leaders of the Kamenev-Zinovyev group in return for public submission to the Party line; and did not even rusticate them. Having control of the secretaries of the Party organization throughout the Union, Stalin was in an exceptional position. The fifteen men who, together with Stalin, form the Politburo therefore govern. There is only one other Politburo in the Union, that of the Ukrainian Communist Party. Its power cannot, of course, be compared to that of the Politburo of the All-Union Communist Party, but it is significant that such a body has been allowed to the second of the two nationalities, Russians and Ukrainians, which possess a political tradition.

The fifteen men of the All-Union Politburo are not all People's Commissars, but have a wide range functions and there are none of the major organs of state in which they are not represented. This is probably inevitable in a centralized state. If the leading personalities in the major organs did not coincide to some extent, i.e. if the leading posts were not covered by a few persons, huge vested powers might find themselves in conflict, with consequent danger to the stability of the State. For example, the Presidium at the head of one pyramid of strength might find itself clashing with Gosplan at the head of another. Furthermore, telephones, wireless telephony, telephoto lines, and air communication have, in recent years, made much less difficult the working of the centralized 'Kremlin control'. The particular type of leadership which Stalin has acquired with the years, leading to the composition of panegyrics to his name, is one which is easily understood by the peoples of Asia. Historically they have been accustomed to the existence of a powerful remote leader. With prominent Russians, the Kremlin and Stalin are more accessible.

Direct control from the centre, intensified, as it were, by the speed of developments in a great State, has involved 'the Kremlin' in an immense strain. Decisions are taken daily on large matters and on minutiae. The lights of the windows beyond the high red wall burn regularly into the early hours. Holidays have been rare for the 'Commissars' over the past twenty years. Hence their country houses and parks are set at no great distance from the capital. As dawn creeps grey-gold over the Kitaiski Gorod and on to the University and the Lenin Library, their low-slung limousines speed out from the Kremlin gates on to the main *chaussées* leading out of town and the forewarned traffic policemen turn the lights to amber ahead of them.

Even with the aid of the Party, which, by definition, must act mainly in a political direction, the Kremlin has to allow much of the social and cultural development of the Union to proceed with its own

momentum. From time to time there are interventions in this or that cultural matter. Shostako-
vich, in the days of a more heavy-handed intervention, was publicly rebuked for his opera *The Lady
Makbeth of the Mtsensk District*. He tottered, but
a smaller man would have fallen. Nowadays such
interventions are a little more avuncular. Ilya
Ehrenburg is slated in *Pravda* by Alexandrov for his
style of writing about Germans. But the hunt does
not follow as the fox slips from covert. Ehrenburg
is writing again.

When Grigori Alexandrov made the comedy film
'*Svetly Put*' (The Happy Road), in which a woman
textile manager makes her maiden speech in the
Supreme Soviet by singing the theme song, the film
was put in cold storage for a time on the grounds
that it was disrespectful of Soviet institutions. A
friend of Alexandrov obtained a showing at the
Kremlin and Stalin reversed the decision saying,
'Our institutions must not be too serious. They
have no strength if we cannot laugh occasionally'. Similarly, Yakovlev, the aircraft designer,
describing in a magazine a series of interviews which
he had with Stalin in the early years of the war,
recounted how he had said to the Premier: 'When I
was a boy, I used to read all the books of Captain
Mayne Reed and Fennimore Cooper. Why don't our
people reproduce them for the young people to-day?'
Stalin, he reports, answered with a chuckle: 'Why?
Oh, there is not enough in those books about
tractors and collectives.' In the 1944 list of books
for young people there was one translated work of
Captain Mayne Reed. These illustrations of modern
interventions in cultural matters are chosen at

random. Nowadays their tendency is more towards
stimulating a livelier approach, where previously
the hold of the political Party over the basic Slav
temperament of the nation had been tight and
serious.

The Party has always been a dogmatic organization. The form of expression which its dogma took
in the years immediately after the Revolution was
some times cumbrous, to a Western mind, and at
others over simple, particularly in matters of history.
But it is a long time since, as is well known, the
cumbrous theory of 'proletarian art' was abandoned
and the school of history which explained the past
entirely in terms of the struggle of classes has been
replaced by the broader pictures of Tarle and
Potemkin. The newer edition of the Soviet encyclopaedia reflects in detail these revaluations of theory
which have been in process for many years. The
Party has also given new emphasis to older traditions and conventions in its recent attitudes towards
the family and to individual, as distinct from
collective, responsibility. Another example of a new
emphasis in its ideas on various fundamentals was
that of an article on 'False ideas in the teaching of
sociology' which was published in the leading
theoretical organ, *Pod Znamenem Marxisma*, in
December 1948. Here it was explained in detail that
it was a gross error to teach that the abolition of
capitalism had done away with economic laws.
There are, went on the article, certain economic
tendencies which in a capitalist economy are allowed
to operate as natural laws; whereas in a Socialist
economy there must be a man-made, man-directed
use of these same economic tendencies. Equally,

dialectical materialism is accepted as the base of Party theory and is taught in the higher schools and universities; but, at the same time, the Orthodox Church with its transcendentalist theology has been allowed to reopen seminaries, and official press organs indicate that the faithful must not be mocked even though their views be ancient. Perhaps it is still too early for anyone outside Russia to attempt a judgment or assessment of many such revaluations or even to recognize a number of them. How, for example, should one assess the fact that nowadays the Party is frequently termed the Party of Lenin-Stalinism? Or what judgment should one make on the importance of the re-emergence of some signs of purely Russian nationalism during the war years, signs going beyond the wearing of St. George Crosses won in the First World War?

Yet most of these revaluations are such as the Russian farmer can understand. Formerly the Communist Party was farther from the countryman. This was not only because its early zest for property in common ran counter to his passionate love of 'veshchi' (things), his craving for personal belongings. The Communist Party was, in origin, a party of the industrial proletariat and proclaimed itself such. Lenin wrote of the Revolution: 'It was made by the proletariat. . . . The proletariat swept along with it the broadest masses of the toiling and poor population.' He also declared at the time, of course, that the Revolution could succeed only if it had the support of the peasants. They did so in order to be rid of landlords. Since then, if the peasant has learned to accept tractors and milking machines, it nevertheless remains true that he has a respect for living and growing things. Throughout Sholokhov's work, and he has always observed his collectivized Cossacks from close at hand, there runs this inherent theme, that some part of the peasant is more concerned with tending the growing thing than with calculating the results. This trait in the peasant has little to do with the aims of an urban Party. But the urban Party has been bound to demand increased production, not for the sake of quality but for the newly teeming towns. Production has had to be the primary demand. Whether the land was thereby treated hardly or not has had to be a secondary matter if millions of mouths were not to go empty. But it is not an accident that a majority of the livestock of the Soviet Union, the rearing of which demands individual care, is still in the possession of the peasantry.

The Party does, however, reach the villages. Through the directors and secretaries of the kolkhozes (collective farms) and through the clubs and libraries and classes which they run, the influence of the Party has stretched out into the countryside. Communists among the personnel of the M.T.S. (machine-tractor stations) have also had a role in bringing Communist doctrine into the countryside. Millions of peasants have learned to read, and in one way or other the national or local press reaches them.

Between the Party and the army the links were originally closer in the revolutionary era than between the Party and the countryside. The young Red Army was largely a revolutionary body. But even in the early days of the new régime the army became consolidated as a distinct function of State

c

power, and many career officers and N.C.O.s threw
in their lot with it as a continuation of their profession. The Party and the army were never fused.
The Party worked in and among the army for
many years. It was represented by the system of
Commissars and 'Politruki' (Political instructors).
Relations between these representatives of the
Communist Party and the regimental officers have
fluctuated. In the battalion or company it was not
always clear whether the active officer or the
political officer held the senior post. For a long time
no order by an active officer was an order on paper
unless countersigned by the political officer. It is
not necessary here to go into detail on the fluctua-
tions in their relationships before 1941. Then, in
the early days of the war, articles began to appear
in the Soviet press insisting that the political officer
should know not only his Communism but also the
tasks of war and set an example as a fighter. Power
of command was reverted to the active officer; and
at the time of Stalingrad the corps of political officers
was disbanded. The Commissars took up, within the
active hierarchy, the ranks for which they were
individually fitted. By that time the Party was
already recruiting in large numbers among those
men of the army who were proven fighters. Sometimes the Party enrolled them immediately after
they had won distinction; sometimes it demanded of
them a few months' probation.

This expansion is symptomatic of the present
position of the Party. Its power remains unchallenged in the peace. Its membership is swollen
with new recruits from the army, from industry, and
the countryside. The Party now reveals a broad

cross-section of the national unity and the increased national consciousness which developed during the four years of heart-breaking struggle. The slogans which the Party of to-day will bring forward are not yet discernible. The ethos which its existent membership will create during the years of reconstruction cannot be foretold.

CHAPTER IV

THE RED ARMY

MUCH more is now known regarding the Red Army than the outside world knew in 1941. An honest observer would admit, however, that it is now more difficult still to describe or assess the armed forces of the Soviet Union. The main picture of their structure has become clearer. On the other hand, there have been so many changes of which a number are still unknown that it would be easy to make many false statements about the Red Army.

The Soviet forces have been reduced by many millions towards a peace-time establishment. The war-time grouping of commands is reverting to the peace-time network. Shortly, the Red Army should have returned to its pre-war form, of a career service to which were attached large annual conscript drafts.

The peace-time standing army was manned at about $1\frac{3}{4}$ millions. During the war, it was expanded to a probable 15 millions. Many of those called up in the first years of the Eastern Front were men of the reserve who had previously served their two or three years as conscripts. The Krasnaya Armiya has, however, acquired a much larger place in the consciousness of the nation than the mobilization of some additional millions of men and large increases in the output of certain arms would imply. The army, as such, has gained a sense of its own importance. At the same time the nation has come to regard the army not as a school in which a man would spend some years of training, but as truly part of its own body.

This confidence and the corporate sense which developed in the army during the war—and which has not been belied by the obvious slackening of discipline in some of the occupation areas of Eastern Europe since the war—has applied both to the regulars and to the enlisted men. For the regulars, the value of such a development is that the blow which their higher ranks took at the time of the 1937 purge has been forgotten. The standards of the military colleges and academies, developed over twenty years, have been vindicated in a struggle with the professional minds of the Wehrmacht. For the enlisted men, the value of the war years lies in the additional personal, practical confidence which they acquired, and especially in their increased confidence in each other.

As regards the structure of the Red Army, little is yet known of the effect of the 1944 amendment to the Constitution which changed the Commissariat of Defence (now named Armed Forces) from an All Union Commissariat to a Union-Republican Commissariat. This change gives the Constituent Republics of the Union the right to concern themselves with their own defence. The republics would, at the same time, be responsible to the Central Commissariat which would supply general guidance on matters of army policy and technique. What effect this will have on the previous territorial commands is uncertain. Before the war the Red Army commands were planned to meet the needs of strategy and mobilization, and not on a republican basis. Thus there existed the First and Second Red

Banner Far Eastern Armies; the First and Second
Central Asiatic Armies; the Caucasus Command; and
the Kiev, Moscow, Minsk, and Leningrad Commands,
or special military districts, etc. The Red Navy
was also centrally directed in the past but its fleets
were naturally dictated by geography. There existed
a Northern Fleet, a Baltic Fleet, a Black Sea Fleet,
including the Dnieper and Don Flotillas, a Caspian
Flotilla, and a Far Eastern Fleet. The Baltic Fleet
is able to maintain a light craft connexion with the
Northern Fleet via the White Sea Canal, and the
Northern Fleet has patiently built up a link with
the Pacific Fleet via the North-East Passage, limited
to a few summer months of ice-free water. The Red
Air Force has, in the past, been still more centralized. It is not an independent command, but works
to the Red Army High Command in much the same
manner as the American Air Force works to the U.S.
Army. As a subsidiary arm dependant from the
army, the Red Air Fleet has specialized as a close-
support force. Still operating in conjunction with
army requirements, its middle-distance striking
power increased gradually during the war. Its long-
distance striking power remained tactical rather
than strategic and did not acquire even the semi-
independent status of the American bomber commands. Stalin has stated that the Red Air Fleet
was backed by an industry which produced a maximum of 40,000 planes a year. It is safe to say that
by far the greater proportion of this production was
devoted to fast fighters, ground-support types such
as the 'Stormovik', and trainers. What modifications will take place in the organization and composition of the Red Air Fleet as a result of the

Constitutional amendment of 1944 are not yet known.

Other sections of the armed forces are the Border Guards, about whose alertness and patriotism much popular literature has been written; the troops of the N.K.V.D. (Commissariat of Internal Affairs), who are organized as military units apart from the police and who showed up well in action; and the coastal defence units, who co-operated with the Northern, Baltic, and Black Sea Fleets. From the beginning of war the Soviet artillery had some independence of action and, from published report, it is obvious that although their mode of operation varied and developed in the course of the war, the gunners tended to be regarded as a distinct arm of war. The existence of Marshals of Artillery, e.g. Nikolai Voronov, is an indication of this tendency. Soviet tank forces acquired a similar homogeneity during the war. Soviet cavalry were used on a divisional scale at the outset of the war, and experience showed that they were not sufficiently integrated with the heavier arms to be able to maintain a line. In the south, on flat or rolling country, the motors of German divisions beat the horse of the Red cavalry in 1941. Throughout 1942 the insistence of Soviet military writers was on the need to weld all types of arms into self-supporting operational units.

Even in the armed forces, the centralism of the Soviet Union shows itself. Towards the end of the war during the great advance westward, the main operational fronts were commanded by Marshals having considerable freedom of manœuvre. Their operations and especially their timing were, however,

ordered by the Supreme Command working inside
the Kremlin to Stalin himself. In the latter part
of the war many of the principal leaders of the
Party had taken military rank, e.g. Shcherbakov as
head of the Political Department of the Red Army
assumed the rank of Lieutenant-General. Some of
the Party leaders had of course previously served
with distinction on the permanent Defence Commission.

Though the outside world knew little of the Red
Army in 1941, it had in fact, for many years, played
a distinctive part in the Soviet way of life. To a
certain extent the army forms part of the life of any
nation which has a traditional conscript system as,
for example, France. But this has been particularly so in the case of the Red Army. In 1919, the
army was clearly a poorly organized collection of
fighting units. Nevertheless, since it was continually
operating on one front or another in an unbroken
stretch until 1924, the Red Army rapidly acquired
some coherence. Despite the bitterness shown in
many places by the revolutionaries towards the
Tsarist officer class, some hundreds of regular officers,
especially those of the technical branches, and still
larger numbers of regular N.C.O.s remained in the
Russian army after the revolutionary campaigns had
been fought and won. At the same time the tradition
of Russian artillery theory and training was maintained in the Academies. The barrage which stunned
von Paulus at Stalingrad and the later rain of fire
which stove in the German centre at Vitebsk were
made possible in 1919 when the historic Russian
interest in artillery was preserved. Although the
Red Army was in action on a local scale on several

occasions before the Finnish campaign of 1940, it had not fought a really large operation until 1941: and yet was not disgraced in its artillery.

The early military understanding reached by the young Soviet republic with Weimar Germany when the two were 'isolated' countries, was of some aid to the Russians in technical matters and the establishment of munition factories. Furthermore, in the arms centres of Leningrad (the Putilov works), Tula, and Moscow, there were experienced workmen with a body of skill in arms-making which only the years can produce.

Upon this basis, much attention was paid to the training and equipment of the Red Army in the years between the wars. Later some of this was shown to be theoretical and unequal to the initial battle experience of the Germans—which was perhaps inevitable since the young Red Army was not launched abroad into offensive experiments as was the revolutionary army of Napoleon's day. The role cast for the Red Army, and the propaganda lines accompanying it, were rather idealistic. For years the Red Army was the defender of the first Socialist State; the first workers' army, which would never battle with the workers and peasants of other lands. As the chances of a Communist China and a Communist Germany faded, and especially after Hitler had manœuvred himself into power, more and more attention was devoted in the Red Army to the military art as such. The Kiev manœuvres of 1935 displayed to the assembled military attachés of many fighting nations the Red Army's large-scale use of tanks, parachutists, and air transport of supplies. These manœuvres were a pointer to the

Russians' later successes in ground-air co-operation.
With the rapid deterioration of the international
position, the army's insistence on the standards of
regular officers became more marked every year.
In 1935, Stalin told the passing-out conference of
Red Army cadet-officers, 'In future, cadres are
everything'. The purge which struck the higher
ranks shortly afterwards shook the army. But
there had always been a gap between the higher
Staff appointments and the Russian 'fighting
colonels', and many of the latter were unaffected by
the purge. Backed by experience in Mongolia and
Finland, a number of such colonels were in divisional
command at the outbreak of the war with Germany.
When I talked with Shcherbakov in 1942 he mentioned the obstacles facing any nation in creating
trained cadres if one had no large body of reserve
officers. In the quiet, firm manner which he had of
compressing realities, he remarked, 'Cadres take
time, Mr. Lovell'. Much work had, in fact, been
done by the Russian High Command in this direction before 1941, especially in the year of respite
after the Finnish campaign. The number of officers
academies had been increased. Officers' clubs had
been founded. Officers had been tested in taking
their men on long operational exercises, particularly
during the winter 1940–41. Lieutenant-General
Ignatyev had been in charge of etiquette and
deportment for officers for some time past and had
revised the classes of foreign languages in the
military colleges.

If in the building of cadres the educational side
of the instruction was important, this was simply a
complement to the general educational function of

the Red Army. For the ranks, the Red Army has
been a school from its beginning. During the two
or three years which a recruit spends with the army,
a definite effort is made to teach him a number of
things other than the right end of a musket. Up
to 1940 there was perhaps too much attention to
political theory in the instruction of the recruit, but
this tendency was reversed throughout 1940 and
1941 to the time of the German attack. The annual
intake of conscripts was inevitably largely of
peasant stock. A fair proportion could read and
write, all these later conscripts being now products
of the Soviet era. The training units were frequently
mixed in racial origin, which was also a civilizing
factor. Despite the fact that the war produced a
Jewish and an Armenian army commander, most of
the higher staff, however, was and had remained
Great Russian. One might say that the Red Army
is one of the main teaching enterprises of the Great
Russians to the smaller brother nations of the
Union. For these smaller nations it was a piece
of immense good fortune that the Red Army staff
consisted to such a large extent of Russians, with a
native military instinct capable of opposing the
formidable professional qualities of the German
staff.

In the early years, as a revulsion from the atmosphere of the Tsarist army, the Red Army worked
in a propaganda climate of international solidarity
of the working-class movements. Increasingly in
the past ten years the accent of its instruction has
been on Russian military tradition and Russian
qualities in battle. Much has already been written
about the restoration of the traditional epaulettes in

their many colours, the reinstitution of Guards units, and the special honour paid to the memory of the historic commanders of former days, Alexandr Nevski, Suvorov, and Kutuzov, during the course of the war. It is interesting, however, to recall that when Timoshenko crashed through the Mannerheim Line in the spring of 1940, he had previously repeated a tactic of Suvorov's. Before the taking of the Bessarabian town of Ismail in 1790, Suvorov caused a replica of the fortress of Ismail to be built with laths and canvas and trained his men in the assault. In 1940, when the strength of the approaches to the Mannerheim Line had been tested, Timoshenko ordered the construction of a system of defences similar to those of the Mannerheim Line at a distance of about fifteen to twenty miles in the rear. Special units were given practice in carrying by assault the systems of defences before they were launched against the Mannerheim Line. This resurrection of an historical approach to a problem is typical of much work which had been done in the Red Army even before the German onslaught in June 1941. During the war the Kutuzov memorial in Leningrad was never without flowers; and as early as 1943 articles were written in Russia describing the earlier Russian capture of Berlin in 1760. A romantic drama on the life and death of Admiral Nakhimov, the defender of Sevastopol in the Crimean War, had been popular in Moscow even before the war. Eisenstein's film, Alexandr Nevski, dealing with the defeat of the Teuton knights at Lake Peipous, was in preparation soon after the middle 'thirties, and he was planning *Ivan the Dread* in the winter of 1940–41.

The restoration in war-time of the orders of
Kutuzov, Suvorov, and Alexandr Nevski, was a
natural development but not one which meant that
the Red Army had lost its earlier character. It did
not mean, for example, that the Red Army had
ceased to be a teaching institution. Probably the
reverse. In peace-time the Red Army had supplied
a vast amount of general education to many millions
of young Soviet men. In building up the technical
branches of a modern army, the Soviet Staff had
to supply men with much information beyond the
scope of the ordinary Soviet citizen's 'seven grades'
of schooling. In the earlier years of the Red Army
many of the conscripts were taught to read and
write, but as time went on it was possible to teach
more of them a great deal of the rudiments of
industry and of scientific agriculture. A three-years'
stay with a well-found army which provided many
opportunities of schooling was, in fact, an additional
education for millions of men. It may be doubted
whether all those from the tiny wooden villages
which were only beginning to change after centuries
of rural isolation, were able to gain the full benefit
of their stay. But the effort put by the State into
the development of the Red Army meant that over
some twenty years it enjoyed a large share in the
country's total economy. Its needs in munitions and
equipment both for strategic and tactical defence
were placed first in the demands on the nation's
resources. The army was well provided with food in
reserve and always ate well. Strategic needs dictated
part of the road-building programme and of railway
construction. A large share of transport and of
the metal output went to the army. Defence needs

determined the location and size of many factories. Even before it had been fully tested in war and had become the darling of the nation, the Soviet army was in a real, material way, 'nasha Krasnaya Armiya' (our own Red Army).

Links between the Red Army and industry have been close since the revolutionary years. This is due in part to the fact that industry was state-owned and could be approached by the Defence Commissariat as our own Royal Arsenal could be approached by the War Office; in part also to the fact that new Soviet industries were continually being created in many areas and of many types, and the army was able to indicate its own needs in design or range of production from the outset. Further-more, Osoaviakhim, the Civilian Defence Organiza-tion, drew its recruits mainly from industry, and of its very nature provided an additional link with the army and air force.

Strong ties also existed before the war between the Red Army and collectivized agriculture. Throughout the 'thirties large numbers of army-trained farmers became leaders of collective farms. Thousands of men trained in tank units became members of machine-tractor stations and vice versa. Soviet cavalry was maintained on a large scale before the war, as also the horse-trains of the Supply units. These branches of the Red Army maintained their links with the sovkhozes (State farms) which are among the principal breeders of horses. Rela-tions between the Red Army and various branches of science in the development of more modern types of weapons and with the chemical industry are obvious, and the links between the army and the

medical profession, which is a State service, were
close from the outbreak of war onward. Even in
peace-time the Commissariat of Health had worked
consistently in close touch with the Red Army.
The Border Guards have a special department concerned with preventing the importation of diseases
by human beings, or animals, or plants. Especially
it collaborates with the Health Commissariat in
warding off from the Union the diseases of Asia.
Long stretches of the Central Asiatic and Mongolian
frontiers are barred by mine-fields and poison
barriers to prevent rodents and other animals from
bringing in plague or other pests.

All these links between the army and the nation
have been strengthened in the past five years, as
is natural in the course of any war. This is also
the case with relations between the army and the
Communist Party. Originally the Party, as the
possessors of power, were suspicious of the army
which, *sui generis*, was also a centre of power.
Hence the institution of the system of political
Commissars which was not only a method of impart-
ing political instruction but also a method of control.
All general orders by officers had to be countersigned by the corresponding 'politruk'. The purge
in the army meant the removal of professional
soldiers who, at a time of crisis, might have been
capable of playing their own power game; whereas
what the Party required was naturally an army
which in the last resort would defend the Party.
When the great test came and the Red Army
gradually held the German drive, the emphasis of
the Party's propaganda within the army was shifted
away from political matters. From 1942 onwards,

articles in *Red Star* and *Pravda* consistently demanded of the politruk that he should not only be
capable of exhorting the rank-and-file but also that
he should inspire by actual skill and heroism in
battle.

Whenever Russia suffered a defeat in the early
stages, there were rumours of treachery. One such
whisper in the first weeks of war was that many
Soviet planes had been lost on the western airfields
through the deliberate negligence of a certain air
force general. Rumours of this sort, however, even
if bandied from mouth to mouth for a few months,
finally fell away into limbo. The higher Party
leadership was automatically just as much concerned
with military matters as was the Red Army Command. The State Defence Committee, the Presidium,
and the Supreme Command, were all primarily
concerned with the organization of victory. Stalin
had much to learn of modern military detail. But
his earlier experience—operational experience during
the revolutionary years, and the conduct of the
campaigns with the Japanese in 1938 and the Finns
in 1940—and his sense of realities aided him to
appreciate rapidly what were military needs. In
1942 it was mentioned in the press that certain
alterations of the divisional structure, especially of
cavalry, were inaugurated as early as October 1941.
Throughout the battle of Moscow, November–
December 1941, it was Stalin who, in working
agreement with higher officers of the Military Command, controlled the use of the strategic reserve,
battalion by battalion. Only military considerations
weighed with Stalin—and Voroshilov and Budenny,
the two essentially Party leaders in the operational

High Command at the beginning of the war, were put to the rear to control the formation of reserve armies.

Only after the failure of the Soviet offensive in the Ukraine in 1942, and the subsequent German break-through at Millerovo leading to the crossing of the Don, was there a moment of flurry. The army had, however, held firm at Voronezh, the great neglected battle of the war, so shielding Tambov and the basic reserve areas east of Moscow. The Party organs, nevertheless, began to cry during a few days for more discipline, and to threaten that certain unit commanders must be taught their jobs, in a manner which suggested that the punitive detachments were already at work. Within a few days, however, the leading articles were back once more on the normal war-time themes of patriotism and national inspira-tion and the army was relieved of this stifling atmosphere in which it would have been difficult to work with confidence. A few weeks later, at the time of the Stalingrad crisis, the 'Veliki Vozhd' (Great Captain), as Stalin was then often called, disbanded the political Commissars and fused them with the army. Meanwhile, in the spring of 1942 the army had been given final control of railway communica-tions. The Party had suffered great losses in man-power in the early stages of the war. It began to enrol thousands from the ranks of the army. This process continued throughout the war so that by 1945 it would have been true to use a chemical analogy and say that: the army of Russia in 1945 was an isotope of the army of 1941, whereas the Party in 1945 was an isobar of that of 1941.

As a means of inspiring the Rear to greater efforts

during the war, links between the Rear and the Red
Army were officially encouraged. Deputations of
workers from factories in the Far Eastern Maritime
province or from the mines of the Urals, or of
kolkhoz leaders, were allowed to make excursions to
troop units in the near-rear of the front. They
brought with them special gifts of war material or
produce from their own districts. Occasionally, a
complete trainload of gifts would be collected from
an entire region and a deputation of leading workers
would accompany the train to the neighbourhood
of the front. In the reverse direction, specialists of
various arms and selected parties from fighting units
visited the factories and explained how the war
material there manufactured had been employed.
These were equally occasions for the handing-over
of collective gifts, which are a more frequent feature
in Soviet life than in the life of the Western powers.
Large numbers of Soviet women were organized in
rotas to visit the hospitals for the purpose of reading
to the wounded or writing their letters. The slogans
of the time were 'Vsyo dlya fronta' (Everything for
the front), 'V tylu kak na fronte' (In the rear as on
the front).

The Soviet Union had been mentally mobilized
and its labour had to a great extent been directed
for many years. The process of moral and intellectual
mobilization for war purposes was easier than in
most other countries. Where there is an absence of
State propaganda in peace-time and a higher average
standard of well-being there is naturally a lag in
securing total moral mobilisation for war. On the
other hand, in the Soviet Union terms of a military
type were being applied to Rear activities almost

immediately after the outbreak of war, e.g. 'trud-front' (labour front), 'frontovye brigady' (front brigades, in the factories). Whereas it took Britain and America longer to acquire such a mentality, when they did so its application was often more efficient. The tendency in the world outside the Soviet Union has been to underestimate the general strain of the war upon the Soviet people and to exaggerate the toughness and single-mindedness of the Soviet individual, especially the Soviet woman. For example, the employment of women in the Red Army and air force has been exaggerated. Very few women, other than those serving with the Partisans, (often a matter of necessity), were allowed in operational units. The trades in which Russian women served were roughly comparable with those of women in Britain in the auxiliary services and in industry. The Russian man has, of course, no greater desire to sacrifice his women in battle than has the Englishman.

The equipment supplied by the Rear to this People's Army in which the average age of the generals is not above forty, need not be described in detail. In most respects it is not peculiar to the Soviet way of life. Weapons especially are not dictated by a political system but by the needs of defensive and offensive. Only one point concerning equipment is proper to this examination, namely, the high standards which the Red Army has tried to maintain for personal equipment. Soviet greatcoats, service boots, valenki (felt boots), winter caps, and the huge 'unty' or fur boots of air-pilots are all of high quality by any international standard. It is not certain whether this standard arises from a

severe system of rejects such as was capriciously
applied to foreign material sent to the Soviet Union
during the war; or whether it arises from a political
motive. The army has been and is, better-found
than the bulk of the population. Both before the
war and up to the present, years of effort have gone
into erecting the army's pride. When the first of the
Guards units were nominated in 1941 they were
those which had particularly distinguished themselves, such as Panfilov's infantry or Dolvator's
light cavalry, or Rotmistrov's tanks. As the Guards
units maintained themselves and established a
tradition they tended to be linked with particular
towns, such as the Preobrazhenski Guards Unit or
the Tula Guards Unit. They were awarded battle
honours in Orders of the Day, which they were
allowed to associate with their own names. The
banner of a Guards unit was handed over with considerable ritual. The commander knelt to receive it
and the unit drawn up in parade order also knelt on
one knee and repeated the oath of the Red Army-
man. The epaulettes which the army donned again
were more imposing in the case of the officers—
whereas at the time of the Revolution the officer's
epaulette had been the typical mark of class distinction and the target of revolutionary displeasure.
The somewhat uniform red-enamelled badges of
pre-war days were replaced by varied ribbons and
decorations. Officers were allowed to have their
batmen, and amusingly enough the traditional
characteristics of the Russian batman rapidly
reappeared. Without the beard and the slowness of
the Tsarist batman, he nevertheless displayed the
same calm, silent, devoted watchfulness. Rules of

etiquette for officers were introduced, such as never to carry parcels or loiter at railway stations. For men, saluting discipline which tailed in the early days of defeat, was reinforced with the growth of self-confidence in the army itself and the traditional Russian manner of reporting to a superior officer not only for the receipt of an order but also to announce its carrying-out was performed with a new smart-ness. This structure of pride—noticeable and worthy of comment only because it was so quickly erected —needs putting into its perspective. The new splendour of the army was to a large extent a reflection of its own increased responsibility. Some writers such as Walter Kolarz have emphasized the reappearance of Russian nationalism and the speed with which the army adapted itself to fit into such a picture. An affection for the historic Russia, how-ever, should not blind one to the fact that the Red Army is led by Soviet generals who are the sons of peasants, of small town school-teachers and iron-foundry men. The Red Army receives drivers from machine-tractor stations and supplies directors to collective farms. It has not become once more the army of Tsarist days. The Party, the socialized industrial system, and the Commissariat of Internal Affairs exist together with it in the same state, so that within the total system of the Union it is *encadrée.*

All the other major branches of Soviet life had been thoroughly tested long before 1941. The Red Army alone had not. Now having survived a great strain it has naturally acquired a stable place in the system. Hence it should not surprise one that in the later part of the war the Suvorov cadet schools were created to provide in a regular flow numbers of the future career officers. Orphans of Soviet war heroes and specially selected boys were allowed to enter these schools, whose uniform, discipline, and ordering of the day resemble the cadet schools of Tsarist times and to whom the nearest parallel in England would be the Royal Naval College at Dartmouth. The career officers which they will become will have a high status in the Soviet Union. During the war the leaders of Russia became impressed with the professional nature of the military art; and this impression is not likely to be weakened by the increasingly scientific character of war. In the case of the Soviet air force, the technical or caste nature of this profession was recognized to some extent before the war. Soviet pilots were well paid, whether engaged on service duties or flying gold back from the Lena region or supplying the depots of Glavsevmorput (Northern Sea Administration). They were sufficiently paid in many cases for their wives not to need to work. The Red Army therefore has come into the peace with the status of its professional men enhanced. For the Red Navy, now administered by the Commissariat of the Armed Forces, a large building programme has been announced which would require the prior establishment of additional new, well-equipped shipyards. To provide the cadres of such an expanded navy, new naval schools are being established. Whatever may be the future importance attached to the political and educational side of the Soviet military service system, Russia as a result of the war is paying great attention to the professional standing of the career men of her army, navy, and air force.

CHAPTER V
GOVERNMENT DEPARTMENTS

WHEREAS the Communist Party has controlled the
Soviet way of life and the Red Army preserved it,
the Government departments or 'the bureaucracy'
have throughout determined its character. The
Russians call these departments as a whole the
'apparat' and any member of them who has become
professionally or bureaucratically conditioned, an
'apparatchik'. In this huge apparatus there are by
now many young Soviet-schooled people of natural
intelligence and a desire to help. Sometimes where
they form the majority of the personnel of a particular office, such as a post office, or an electricity
department, one will find a small island of particular
efficiency in this vast slow-moving stream.

The Commissariats as it will still be convenient to
call them in this book, cover all the usual activities
of a community, from fishing to education, from
defence to the wood industry. In addition they have
to supervise the carrying out of innumerable plans
which dovetail to form a total plan. For the past
fifteen years the community as a whole has been set
an objective, a target which receded as the nation
advanced. Within the nation, individual private
initiative is not proscribed and consequently there
are large numbers of private peasants and individual
craftsmen who have no target and do not share
deliberately in the nation's planning. They are
heavily taxed but otherwise they are free to carry
on their own businesses provided they do not employ

other labour. Only the State is allowed to exploit—
in the French sense of the word—the labour of
others. By 1938 not more than five per cent of the
national economy of the Soviet Union was the result
of individual private enterprise.

Planned economies have been partly operated elsewhere, notably in Germany, where planning was a
corollary of the autarchy willed by Hitler. In the
Soviet Union, on the assumption of a socialized
economy, planning was inevitable. When once the
proletarian revolution had been achieved and consolidated against external opposition, the national
economy had to be restored at least to its original
momentum. This was accomplished by means of the
period of the New Economic Policy (N.E.P.) in
which under concessions capable of control by the
State, capitalist enterprise was permitted. But so
soon as the national economy had been more or less
restored, the question from 1928 onward was what
to do with the means of production now owned by
the State. Whereas a capitalist concern could expand
in accordance with the market, the Socialist State
had to set itself an objective for its industry and its
agriculture. Only thus, faced with the needs of
Russia, could the State fulfil the responsibilities
which it had accepted. And once a Plan had been
inaugurated, the populace had to fulfil the task.
Furthermore, since State ownership existed throughout the Soviet Union, the task had to cover the
entire Union in all its activities. It is possible to
describe this series of plans by saying that 'the
nation launched itself into the assault against lack
of steel or X or Y or Z'. On the other hand, it
is perhaps better to examine this development

objectively and even mechanistically. The advent of
the Revolution had greatly increased the kinetic
energy of Russia as a whole, and no one who has
spent any length of time in Russia could doubt that
this was so. The effect of planning has been to
translate the increased energy into additional mass.
The total, quantitatively, of production, consumption, and utilization within the State has risen.
Consequently for the average individual this has
meant expending more energy in more directions.
Those directions are to a large extent prescribed or
planned. The efficiency with which the citizen has
expended his energy is, of course, another matter.
The plans have had to take account of his average
efficiency and have been set so that they could be
fulfilled.

The volume of experience which this system has
given not only to the planners but also to the planned
is unequalled in any other state. This probably
accounts for the extreme sensitiveness to criticism,
not only on the part of the Soviet State or its
leaders but also of the average articulate Russian.
Even where the Russian feels that the foreigner
whom he has met is not unfriendly, he is in many
cases inclined to take the attitude: 'We alone know
what we have done and in what circumstances.
You who come from outside could not understand
and therefore hardly have the right to speak.'

To carry out the system described above, there exist
in the administration two parallel mechanisms, the
Planning bodies, and the Commissariats. The Planning Commission (Gosplan) is ultimately responsible
to the Council of People's Commissars. Nevertheless, the Chairman of Gosplan, M. Voznesenski,

having an overall picture of the economy of state is in a privileged position. It is open to him to criticize the working of various undertakings or branches of administration which come within the province of this or that Commissariat. When M. Voznesenski spoke to the Communist Party Congress in February 1941, he was not sparing in his criticisms of the Soviet metal industry—condemning parti-cularly wastage of metal which lay around in the factory yards.

The process of planning is highly complicated. A volume of evidence exists that in many branches planning was a 'hit or miss' affair during the first five-year period. But the fourth plan which has been started with the peace is developed from a con-siderable body of experience. A network of planning commissions exists whose duty it is to collect the relevant data making up the plan for the whole Union. The various constituent and autonomous republics have their own planning bodies working to their own Councils of Ministers. Regional and republican schemes of economic development are worked out locally. The State Planning Commission governing the whole development of the Union has the last word and is aided by a number of research institutes. Estimates are supplied by all govern-mental bodies covering not only industry and agriculture but also all other activities within the State from the arts to defence. When the plan has been established for the year it is split up into quarterly plans and each quarterly plan can be examined before it begins to operate and modified where necessary. As a planning system has been in force in the Soviet Union for a number of years, it is

possible for the planning authorities to draw up
each year a provisional plan for the following twelve
months, on the basis of an immense amount of data.
The provisional plan has to be approved by the
Council of Ministers after which it is subject to
minor amendment before it comes into force. At the
provisional stage the plans are of necessity linked
up with the financial and credit estimates of the
Union. The finance plan is strictly controlled and
the evidence of recent years tends to suggest that the
Commissariat of Finance has just as much authority
in the matter of estimates as has the British
Treasury. What is certain is that when the Supreme
Soviet meets and the Minister of Finance presents
his annual budget, there is considerable discussion
in committee among delegates from the various
republics anxious to increase the size of their local
budgets by additional grants for education, health,
etc.

Implementation of the Soviet plans falls to the
Commissariats which are roughly speaking of two
categories. Firstly, there are those government
departments directly responsible for a branch or
State activity throughout the whole Union.
Secondly, there are those which operate indirectly
through the respective Commissariats of the constituent republics. The distinction between the first
category, All-Union People's Commissarjats, and the
second, Union-Republican People's Commissariats,
is defined in Articles 75 and 76 of the Constitution.
There are 22 Commissariats in the first category and
18 in the second, though those dealing with coal,
oil, and building have been recently sub-divided on
a regional or functional basis:

1. Foreign Trade, Railways, Posts, Maritime Fleet, River Fleet, Mining Industry, Oil Industry, Electric Power Stations, Electrical Engineering, Iron and Steel Industry, Non-Ferrous Metals Industry, Chemical Industry, Aircraft Industry, Ship-Building Industry, Munitions Industry, Armaments Industry, Heavy Machine-Building, Medium Machine-Building, General Machine-Building, Agricultural Stocks, Building, and the Cellulose and Paper Industry.

2. Armed Forces, Foreign Affairs, Food Industry, Fishing Industry, Meat and Dairy Produce Industry, Light Industry, Textile Industry, Timber Industry, Agriculture, State Grain and Livestock Farms, Finance, Trade, Internal Affairs, Justice, Public Health, Building Materials Industry, and State Control.

Thus with the exception of the subjects mentioned in the first category, the republics of the Union are granted considerable powers, not merely regarding secondary matters but in all domestic affairs. From the lists of Commissariats which I have given it is clear, however, that the relative importance of government departments varies considerably. There is necessarily a wider variation than in other countries where State direction of the national economy is more limited. The picture I have given is the picture at this moment, but it has to be remembered that the Commissariats, local and central, have changed frequently in the past twenty-five years. For example, in 1935 the functions of the Commissariat of Social Welfare passed entirely to the trade unions. In the development of the present picture one constantly recurring problem has been how to resolve the diverging tendencies of the centralism of the régime and the regionalism necessary to the economy of a continent.

Perhaps because of its day-to-day concern with the practical affairs of State, the 'Sovnarkom' (Council of Ministers) has an immediate importance in the minds of the people. It is tangibly a Government whereas the Party is not an ordinary political party, and the Supreme Soviet is not an ordinary debating chamber such as other countries possess. The 'Sovnarkom' or rather its individual members may be criticized. Its building in the centre of Moscow is approachable, being outside the Kremlin. Furthermore, a number of dependent Commissions or bodies are attached to, or work directly to, the 'Sovnarkom', e.g. the news agency Tass, the Commission of Fine Arts, and a number of scientific organizations.

The principal subjects which the 'Sovnarkom' does not directly control but which are in the hands of the republics are not minor 'cultural' activities but some of the major branches of administration. Prominent among them is education, which in the effervescent state of the Soviet Union is not merely a routine conveyance of knowledge but is essentially linked with the economy itself. Health is another Union-Republican subject; which is probably dictated by the wide variation of climates, of endemic disease, etc. It would be hazardous to state why finance is another of these subjects—but perhaps the reason is that it affords the sixteen republics a basic schooling in one of our own aspects of democracy. 'No taxation without representation' was one of the earliest slogans aiding in the birth of our own democracy. The two other important non-reserved subjects, armed forces, and foreign affairs, have been allowed to the Constituent Republics very recently. They can still be regarded only as a further opportunity to the nationalities to acquire experience and additional education in local responsibility. In the matter of foreign affairs some seven of the Constituent Republics are already beginning to build small cadres for the conduct of diplomacy, this being typical of the Soviet sense of priorities. Already delegations from the Ukraine and White Russia have attended the UNO Conferences in San Francisco and London, and the Paris Peace Conference.

Within the Council of Ministers there have been numerous personal changes in the course of twenty-five years. There have not necessarily been more changes than in other countries where Ministers fall with a change of government. More attention is naturally paid by the outside world to the fall of one or other of the Soviet 'giants'. Actually, some Russian departments have had a longer tradition of office than others. Some have of their nature proved easier to adapt to a complete Socialist economy than others, e.g. the police has proved easy while fishing has proved difficult, wood has proved manageable while light industry has been halting. Success or failure on the part of any department within a planned economy quickly reflects itself in the rise or fall of its leaders. Criticism gradually mounts regarding this or that Commissariat because of the interlocking responsibilities of all the other Government departments which are servants of a Socialist State. Furthermore, the administration can be criticized whereas the Party or the régime cannot be attacked except by the imprudent. As a result it is criticized; and often the criticism comes into the public press—after remedial steps have already been taken.

Among those Commissariats the importance of which has grown is the Finance Commissariat. By experience it has been proved that planning and the budget must go hand in hand, and whichever Commissariat is linked with the Planning Commission is automatically powerful. Within the framework of the system of communal ownership of the means and methods of production, Soviet finance has become stabilized and conventional in the sense that the credit system is carefully controlled and individual undertakings or branches of the economy are expected to become self-supporting or profit-making wherever possible. Since the central Government has strictly and determinedly enforced a policy of securing a value to money, State factories or republics have to fight on occasion to obtain larger expenditures and are expected to justify their expenditures by results. In other words, money is not regarded simply as a necessary lubricant for the State machine.

Where an enormous amount of capital development is in progress, a complicated credit system must of course be devised. In the Soviet Union a large proportion of the nation's energies has been devoted to capital development. The necessary credit system could be controlled only if the monetary system possessed some stability. So far as an outside observer can determine there appear to be three interlocking currents or flows of credits in Russia, which might be held to represent the existence of three roubles, i.e. three internal values. These currents of credit apply roughly to: raw materials; the processing system; and consumption. As control lies with the State, the price subsidies necessary in the transfer of goods from one of the three circulations to another can be borne on the State's currency system with some buoyancy. At the same time it is essential to the maintenance of a stable monetary policy in the Soviet Union that the State should recover a large proportion of its outflow of credit by an inflow of money through loans and especially through the turnover tax. In addition, State enterprises have to pay part of their profits back to the State.

During the war many indications of Soviet financial method were given simply by the manner in which the Government chose to meet the stresses of the war situation. For instance, the Soviet financiers strove firmly to maintain a policy of money-value even when consumption goods were scarcest. Barter was not allowed officially even in the 'free market'. In the early days there were numerous arrests of peasants and other free-market traders who were caught indulging in barter or other deals where the passing of money was really fictitious. Another example lies in the fact that when wages rose rapidly with the war drive at piece-work rates, a policy of loans and savings was carried out which was similar in many ways to that employed in Britain for the financing of the war and the prevention of inflation. In Russia the authorities began this process with a lottery loan in which it was possible to win prizes such as a pair of shoes or a caracal coat. Such enticements were rapidly abandoned so soon as the volume of patriotic saving became apparent;

and the peasants began to unload their roubles, stored in some cases over many years, into the funds for tanks and aircraft. So soon as it was evident that victory was a matter of time only, special shops were opened to sell the few luxury goods available, at fantastic prices, and thus still further to pull in the war inflation currency.

The State having complete control of foreign trade, the Finance Commissariat has been able to nominate a gold value for the external rouble. This has been maintained both against the pound and the dollar, and without variation even at the time when Russia's fortunes looked grimmest. In peace-time Russia could always set whatever price she wished, even an uneconomic price, upon the commodities she wished to export in order to obtain foreign exchange to meet her purchases of foreign goods. In the calculations involved, her Government chose to give the rouble a certain gold value, which sets it at a very high rate compared with the pound or the dollar. This value bears no relation to the internal purchasing power of the rouble in commodities and still less in consumption goods. However, the fact is that the rouble can have all the backing in gold which it might ever require for the real volume of Soviet external exchanges. Even before the war the Union was probably the second largest gold producer in the world and there is reason to suppose that her annual production has increased since then.

The three Commissariats which have borne the great strain of the period of Soviet economic expansion are: Communications, Railways, and the River Fleet. All three have received their meed of criticism from time to time in the State press. Any

D

failure on their part to meet the demands of the Planning system is more immediately obvious than is the case with other Commissariats. At the same time the total of freight hauls and passenger journeys on the railways; the volume of letter and telegram traffic; the Russian indulgence in telephoning; and the size of water-borne traffic have all increased enormously throughout the past twenty-five years. The overall length of railways lines has increased comparatively slowly, also the estimated total of available wagons. But these figures are in fact no criterion. It seems true to conclude that the equipment of the railways has been used by an increasing volume of traffic without regard to the working life of the equipment. Much of the material of the Commissariats mentioned is overloaded and the standards of their technical equipment are uneven. The movement of millions of people into Asia; the movement of millions of country people into the cities; these and a number of other major changes within the Union have caused a drastic overburdening of communications throughout more than twenty years. It is significant that Stalin and Kaganovich have announced that the first post-war five-year plan is due to rectify this situation by the building of new railways, wagons, etc.

Civil air lines form the one communications service which has developed comparatively rapidly. The Aeroflot company has taken tips from foreign services, especially Lufthansa with which it operated conjointly on certain services in its early stages. The company has also experimented considerably and possesses altogether a respectable fleet principally of Soviet-built craft of Douglas design. It is not uncommon to see persons of all grades of employment travelling by air, from high Party officials to the wives and children of army captains. How all these people manage to travel is not clear since a system of priorities has operated in recent years. It is a fact, however, that the prices are reasonable compared with the total costs of railway travel, which in a country as large as the Soviet Union is necessarily lengthy and expensive beyond the actual cost of the ticket.

Perhaps it is trite to emphasize again that all the Commissariats and the network of communications have to work in the local circumstances of many different climates and among different peoples. Russian railways operate in Russia as British railways operate in Britain and French railways in France. Equally, the achievements of any given Commissariat which gain great publicity or other attention in Russia do·so because they have been won in Russia. A section of the agricultural exhibition in Moscow provided an example of this in 1941. Many three-quarter-ton and other lorries for use in country districts were on view and a high proportion of them had equipment so that they could be driven on spirit produced by burning wood. These lorries were proudly displayed in an exhibition, because they were most practical for a country where much wood is available and is a cheap fuel although the same country produces millions of tons of oil. In the same way it is possible to judge the work of the mines administration only against the background of the inaccessibility of many of the development areas, the difficulty of attracting skilled personnel to these areas and conveying materials and building homes for the workers during the long winter, etc. A number of other facts have to be understood not only in their geographical but also their historical perspective. Among these are the part which women are now playing in the professions, the care of pregnant women and young children. In the liberalizing movements of Russia, women have traditionally played a considerable role and it is not surprising that following upon the Revolution large numbers of Russian women should have taken advantage of the new opportunities offered to them. On the other hand, in Central Asia the pressure of the Soviet authorities to secure special care for expectant mothers has meant a sudden break with the past centuries. The structure of the Soviet system of Commissariats is therefore not to be divorced from the country and the people in which it has to function. For a proper appreciation of its achievements and failures both the system and its people must be viewed together.

The forty-five Commissariats and their counterparts in the Constituent Republics cover the whole field of life in the Union. Quite apart from those of the various industries and agriculture, the many Commissariats are a necessity to the Soviet way of life and its planned economy. Their multiplicity, of course, involves a large number of officials. Before the Revolution Russia had had some experience of officialdom, and the Soviet leaders have been obliged to build largely on this experience. Tsarist bureaucracy had its own peculiarities and many of them are repeated among the 'apparat' of to-day. There is the inherited worship of forms, of stamps and signatures; the magic validity of the stamped document·

While all this is true, there has been a desire to improve upon the 'chinovnik', the minor official of Tsarist days. The Press has campaigned once in every year or eighteen months against the ways of the bureaucrat. The campaign in the winter of 1943–4 was especially long, and many cases were quoted of 'indifference and callousness'. Such campaigns are usually accompanied by a number of well-publicized prison sentences *'pour encourager les autres'*. The common faults of bureaucracy are known throughout the world. The worst aspects of the Soviet variety derive from the rapid conversion of many thousands of former peasants, servants, and semi-skilled workers into officials. This fact, taken together with the stern responsibilities imposed by the system, results in a rigidity, an anchylose quality, in the bureaucracy here and there which involves a permanent percentage of drag in the machine. As the level of general education rises, a greater degree of suppleness will no doubt be acquired. The new generation which is gradually taking over the working of the machine talks in terms of 'Stalinist technique', by which it means a peremptory but alert efficiency.

Among the higher bureaucrats or administrators one finds that they have by experience an extraordinarily rapid appreciation of priorities. The necessities of building a great deal in a short time have so deeply inculcated this sense of priorities that its mode of application is sometimes inhumane. For example, certain of the new factories in the Far East were erected and a labour force for them collected before adequate living conditions in the extreme climate had been created. The systems of priorities worked out by the individual Commissariats can result in a clash of interests, or rival claims on commodities. A legal system exists to regulate such clashes, but inevitably disputes are often decided by the personalities of the leaders concerned. This leads to the formation throughout the system of a political 'gun-power' rating, and weaker personalities on such a rating go to the wall.

Over a long period the volume of work of the Commissariats has continuously expanded. Soviet life has become more complex as a result of much experimentation. The citizen has seen this and that branch of the administration try out many methods, e.g. in agriculture, in education, in light industry. In a great bustle the administration has practised experimental surgery upon the people and upon itself. The Russian citizen has not been and is not completely passive under such administration. His methods of reacting or criticizing are not British methods and would require a lengthy explanation. Broadly, they take two forms. On the negative side they may take sometimes the form of a sullen Slav resistance. On the positive side the citizen, who is by definition part-owner of the State, can express his annoyance by joining in the collective, officially encouraged 'samokritika' (self-criticism). In beating his own and the collective breast at a factory or office meeting he is also, in a peculiarly Russian way, belabouring the hide of the administration.

CHAPTER VI
SECURITY

THE Soviet country and people are being renewed in one sense by the huge governmental apparatus which I have described; and at a furious tempo. Whether Utopia or not, it is a system with a purpose. This system has been in operation for nearly thirty years following a bloody Revolution, the execution of the reigning family, and the defeat of prolonged attempts at intervention by Powers whose subjects had invested large sums in Russia. The experiment has also involved the creation in less than a generation of an industrial working class of many millions. These latter are breadwinners but not bread makers. To meet this situation the system of agriculture has been drastically converted, with the accompanying elimination of one class of the rural community and the deportation of millions from this kulak class to new areas of settlement. During the greater part of the post-revolutionary period a struggle over fundamental policy went on within the ruling party. The struggle, principally against Left elements, was not resolved until 1937 although won by Stalin's group in principle as early as 1927. Thus through nearly thirty years the Russian State has lurched forward like a great stage-coach, swaying and creaking, the leather springs straining. Insecurity from abroad added to internal travail have rolled across the material hazards of Russia.

Such insecurity has two results: its effect upon the ruling party and its effect upon the State.

Counter-measures are taken to secure the continuity
of the Party and to ward off possible threats to the
continuity of the State. Inevitably this has caused a
special importance to be given in the Soviet Union to
those organs of the State which are concerned with
security. The first consideration of the Soviet
Government has been to preserve the experiment
which it was carrying out. In such a situation the
development of a tradition or of conscious stability
within the organs of security takes time. The Soviet
security system was born in an atmosphere of
suspicion in order to defend a Revolution. And
suspicion breeds upon itself. In the Soviet Union
the search for security down all the corridors of
suspicion led finally to the period of neurosis of
1934–7; the neurosis of the trials and the purge.
When in early 1938 Stalin and the Party of Russia
at last shed the hysteria, the whole forest around
them had been thinned. Most of the great pines
were down.

From outside it is difficult to appreciate this complex of the 'search for security'. Much reading of
the Soviet press (for the whole post-revolutionary
period) and of the verbatim record of the great
trials of Zinovyev, Rykov, Bukharin, and Radek,
is necessary if one is to begin to understand the super-
sensitiveness of the Soviet State, its harshness and
swiftness of repression. However, the simple fact
for the observer is that within the Soviet way of life
'security' is a constant factor.

The organs of State security have had to operate
in a land some 7,000 miles long by 4,000 broad.
With a highly centralized system to defend, they
have had to be as effective at Vladivostok as at

Bokhara and Archangel. They have had to maintain their grip upon many distinct races; and especially upon the race of Great Russians, historically given to conspiracy and the formation of secret societies. The Soviet security organs watch over a country which has had a tradition of assassination. The landmarks in Russian history were often the shudders upon the earth as the Tsars and their favourites fell. Hence it was well within the context of the Russian history that the reaction of the State should have been so fierce, when in 1934 danger came as near to the centre of power as Leningrad, where it struck down Stalin's chief local representative, Kirov. Furthermore, the communications of the country have been developing only gradually throughout three decades against great obstacles of rivers and mountains and extremes of climate. This has meant that the task of the organs of security has been lightened slowly. It is interesting to note therefore that the most satisfactory method of control has been found to lie in a Union-Republican Commissariat and not in an All-Union Commissariat.

Some form of police exists in every State. The police is a necessary organ with a wide range of responsibilities. Every normal citizen accepts the police of his own State. But there is always a tendency for the citizen of one State to exaggerate the repressive or even the normal activities of control by a foreign police. Many exaggerated notions concerning the American police system, for example, have been current in England. In particular, the American police have been represented as a body of strong-arm men, and the American local tradition, which tends to represent the typical beatman as a

middle-aged Irishman with an affection for found-
lings, has been ignored. Equally, many distortions
have been current regarding the Soviet organs of
security. Many aspects of the work of the N.K.V.D.
(Commissariat of Internal Affairs) which are normal
to any police system have been made to appear
sinister or have been ignored entirely, with the
result that the outside world sees the picture lop-
sided. In other words, the police also directs traffic.

What is really of interest in examining the work
of a police force is the extent to which such work is
in evidence, i.e. is the normal visible work laboured,
or is the covert work carried out repressively so as
to create a continuous atmosphere of uncertainty?
In drawing up such an assessment, the judgment of
a foreigner is probably of little value. As it seems to
me, this is particularly true in the case of the Soviet
system. The foreigner has a special régime in Russia.
No attempt is made by the authorities to conceal the
fact that he is apart, that he is not 'nash' (one of us).
The result is that many foreigners in Russia attribute
their own reactions to the ordinary Soviet citizen—
when, in logic, this is by no means necessarily the
case. It may be that the Russian reacts to the
atmosphere of his surroundings in the same way as
the foreigner, but not necessarily so. In addition,
the foreigner is hindered in making a true assessment
by the following fact. The attitude of the Soviet
authorities to Russians who come in contact with
foreigners is governed by the very fact of that
contact. In other words, what the foreigner cannot
know is the atmosphere of life among ordinary
Russians, let us say in the provinces, who have no
contact with foreigners.

From the point of view of the Russian State, contact with foreigners usually has a demoralizing effect upon the local citizen. This is true not only of our own day. One has only to read Russian history in a little detail to realize that the Russian attitude to foreigners has for centuries been much the same as to-day. Queen Elizabeth's first Ambassador to the Court of Muscovy had to wait three weeks in Moscow to obtain his first audience with the ruling duke. The very isolation of Russia during the centuries has also meant that whenever Russians came into lengthy contact with foreigners they tended to absorb not the domestic virtues common to Russia but exaggerations of taste or of style, or to accept as conventions Western fads of the moment. Again, one has only to read the history of the censorship in Russia in the nineteenth century (for instance, M. Lemke's book on this subject, *St. Petersburg*, 1904) to realize that censorship lies in the tradition of the country, although the form of the censorship might vary considerably from one period to another. Equally, the tradition has existed in Russia of an outward-looking group opposing an inward-looking or Russian group. At times this opposition has formed one of the major political issues of the day, as for example in the closing decades of the nineteenth century, when the Russian group fought a running fight with the 'zapadniki' (Westerners).

But to return to the question of security in modern Russia: before trying to estimate how the search by the State for security impinges upon the Soviet individual it is necessary to consider the organs through which the State works. There are two main bodies. These have at times been completely separate and at other, as at present, combined into one Commissariat. The N.K.V.D. comprises not only the normal policing and control sections of any such government department, but also the Unified State Political Department. The former department is concerned with all the usual tasks of a police force and certain others which are incidental to the Soviet system, such as control of internal passports and registration. The latter, or Unified State Political Department, derives from the political system of the Union, which it is designed to protect. And as a consequence it also has its links with the outside world.

The militia are the instruments of the Commissariat proper. The technique of this blue-uniformed police is not that of the London 'bobby'; but it is one which in its surroundings is understood. Among its functions are: traffic control, the arrest of drunks, protection against burglary and links with 'domkomy' (house committees), control of the free markets and the maintenance of order among crowds. In general, the attitude of the public is sympathetic to the militiaman. Occasionally a citizen will voice his dislike of being fined on the spot for crossing the street at the wrong place; or a crowd will shout its annoyance should a militiaman do the rare thing and use any violence in picking up a drunk, because they do not consider that the Revolution was intended for that purpose.

The political section of the Commissariat is partly uniformed, partly in plain clothes. It is highly sectionalized, which has sometimes in the past led to bitter struggles of competence; and as its name suggests, the department is ubiquitous, from the street corner to the factory meeting. The uniformed sections of the department appear to grade away from routine police work into the army; and those in plain clothes to grade away from normal detective work into the Party.

There are many ways of regarding the work of such a government department. But in any case it may be said that from 1938 onwards when Beriya, the Georgian, took over the Commissarship, one intention of both sections of the department has been to help in the civilizing process of the Soviet system. They have aided in the development by control or conditioning of 'kulturnye lyudi' (civilized people, to translate freely). The various republics, which have control of their own police, consist of races at widely different levels of civilization. To raise these to a common higher level rapidly automatically involves a considerable measure of control. In addition, the police are faced from time to time with waves of crime in various localities—especially because so many millions of people have been moved about the country. The amount of petty theft also varies from district to district. Banditry was still a problem in Central Asia, especially on the outskirts of the rapidly growing towns, as late as the end of the 'thirties. Juvenile delinquency was a great problem in the early 'thirties at the time when gangs of homeless children amounting in all to some hundreds of thousands were roving the countryside. This problem was solved during the 'thirties by putting these youngsters to work, and by the occupational schools; but the war which has taken the lives of so many parents has renewed the problem to some extent in those areas which were overrun by

the Germans. To all these factors, demanding altogether a large police activity, must be added the fact
that in a fully socialized state much property is
communally owned, and thus has to be guarded by
the organs of the community.

Defence of the State itself is shared by the State
Political Department and the Communist Party, and
on the highest personal levels these organizations
merge. But upon the ordinary citizen of the Soviet
State is placed the duty to report any facts which
may in any way endanger the State. Any Englishman has the same duty *vis-à-vis* his own State,
otherwise he may find himself an accessory after the
fact. The question is how such a duty shall be interpreted. In the Soviet Union at certain times it has
been interpreted in an absolutist manner, and people
have been sent to hard labour for not reporting facts,
the significance of which they did not understand.
Gradually, however, since 1938 some small tradition
of logic and an incipient sense of tolerance have
begun to develop. Not all who have an accident with
valuable machinery are now 'wreckers'. Not all
who fail to achieve a target figure which has been set
too high are 'counter-revolutionaries'.

The responsibility devolving on the Party for
defending the State is, of course, still higher. This
problem may also be considered resolved—but the
outside world tends to forget that the battle of
policies within the Party was long and keen, and was
conducted by 'giants of Revolutionary technique'.
Suvarin's book on Stalin should not be read in order
to obtain a favourable impression of the Soviet
Union, but it is a good indication of the fierceness of
the inter-Party struggle. It is foolish to assume that

the opposition of Trotski, Zinovyev, Kamenev,
Bukharin, etc., was not bitterly conducted, and
cleverly. Where in a normal Parliamentary régime
the battle would have been fought with words on
the floor of the Chamber, in the Soviet Union this
could not occur because of the ideological basis of
the proletarian state. Instead the fight was conducted
in the Party cells and in the factory clubs to the
point where finally 'down with Stalin' was being
woven secretly into the pattern of men's neckties.
Had the Opposition won against Stalin's group the
victory would have been just as much a revolution
as any other, even though it occurred inside one
particular Communist Party. And here again it is
necessary to stress that the battle within the State
over its régime has been conducted in a Russian
atmosphere, with Russian methods. From the point
of view of the organs of security these methods have
simply become more scientific, more 'psychological'
rather than material. Probing by keen and prolonged
questioning has replaced the knout. Evidence on
such a matter must be difficult to obtain. But the
consensus of normally well-informed opinion is that
torture has not been used since the days of Yagoda's
Commissarship, and even then it would have been
abnormal. The advance to the scientific method of
examination came significantly under the madman
Yezhov, who later perished as Yagoda had done.
The State trials arising out of the struggle within
the Party were, as I have mentioned earlier, largely
a revelation of devotion to the Party; and the
notorious 'confessions' only to be understood inside
the ethos of Russia itself. It would be possible to
enlarge on this theme. But probably only a Russian

could appreciate fully how behind the pitiable, maudlin self-accusations sounded an orchestra of frustrated Russian hopes, of weakness through division, of decades of clanking chains throughout Siberia.

The power of the police in the Russian Empire; the early curious links between the Party and the police as a measure of self-protection; the respect of the 'Okhrana' (Tsarist secret police) for the skill of the Bolsheviks and their elaboration of secret method— some understanding of all this is necessary to an assessment of how the State Political Department has developed. In the same way that many of the traditions and much technique of the former Russian Army were retained in the Red Army, so many of the habits of police control by the 'Okhrana' were taken over by the State Political Department. In fact the days of the old revolutionary 'Cheka', with its partly indiscriminate violence, were relatively short. Soviet police methods became prophylactic rather than correctionary. Whether this was due to a gradual assumption of more power by the retained personnel of the old professional police, or whether a new generation took control, it is difficult to state with any certainty. The latter hypothesis is probably true in the case of the N.K.V.D. guards, a Soviet development, and those sections on a junior level who have to deal with foreigners.

A special part is played in the Soviet way of life by the organs of security. To a greater extent than the similar organs of other powers, the police of the Soviet Union aids in 'lubricating' the system. For example, they maintain a watch on communications, especially the railways, which is only partly a police activity. This watch is also largely a matter of fostering efficiency. The presence of police in various other State institutions is equally only partly a means of preventing these institutions from becoming focal points of any disaffection. The control of efficiency is an additional reason for their presence.

The N.K.V.D. through its various agencies in the Union controls altogether a large body of labour. In the development of outlying areas, in the construction of essential works in the most unpleasant physical conditions, this body of labour has been of great value in Russia and in Asia. To gloss over the human misery which is in the charge of this department would be foolish. To ignore the extent to which the early idealistic schemes of the Revolutionary correctional system have been abandoned or malformed, would be dishonest. Stupidity among the lower personnel is probably the determining factor.

The actions of the N.K.V.D. are subject to approval by the Soviet courts, and ultimately by the Supreme Court. Furthermore, these actions are taken in application of the criminal and civil codes. Hence there is a juridical basis for the methods of the police. But the actual scope of the police is not easy to determine. Their relations with the border guards, and on the military side with the Red Army, are difficult to define. The links, however, are visibly close, and some members of the higher body of Soviet attorneys assumed military rank during the war and took a leading part in courts martial.

The Soviet Union's courts for the application of the criminal and civil codes are built up firstly on a republican and secondly on an All-Union basis, so that their structure is similar to that of the Soviets and the Commissariats. Judges and the 'people's assessors', who sit on every bench, are elected, and the judiciary is under the Constitution independent of the administration. However, the wide scope given to the militia and the Political Department results in the judiciary lacking the public prestige of its British counterpart. Public attendance at the courts, where permitted, is rare; and only on the criminal side of the law are a certain number of lawyers well known. The universities have, of course, faculties of law, and disputes among Soviet institutions and among the Commissariats do provide briefs for barristers and solicitors. The status of the Soviet equivalent of solicitors was not high in the years following the Revolution. Later the consolidation of Soviet professional groups, the creation of a more complex society, and successive modifications of the inheritance law have produced an increased care for the rights of private property, and the status of the solicitor has tended to rise. At the same time non-political crimes, such as murder or robbery with violence, are nowadays treated more severely than was the case in the idealistic early years of the Union. Laws concerning the sexes have been strengthened. Since the anti-abortion law of 1937 the maintenance of the family has been protected by two changes in the divorce laws. This development has been accompanied by measures tending to make marriage a more solemn occasion. The civil registry offices in which they take place are nowadays decorated with flowers and the presiding official often addresses a few words of advice to the newly married couple.

On the criminal side of the law there have not been

such changes in Soviet times as on the civil side. The criminal law has remained stable. It is not based on Roman-Dutch law, but according to a Soviet official statement 'is based on a logical and consistent materialism'. 'The body of Soviet criminal law is an integral part of the policy of the workers' State . . . and serves as a weapon against the enemies of the proletariat. In the second place the criminal law of the Union is intended to foster a spirit of social discipline and self-discipline in the ranks of the working class.' The criminal code is divided into two parts, Union and Republican. Crimes also fall into two categories. The first includes those directed against the Soviet order itself and for that reason regarded as the most dangerous; the second comprises all other crimes. The determination of the various crimes and the manner in which correction or punishment is to be applied, come within the jurisdiction of the Constituent Republics, except in cases of treason or military offences, both of which can be judged only in All-Union courts. While the criminal law itself has not been fundamentally changed with the consolidation of Soviet society, nevertheless there have been many changes in the method of application. These changes have been the result of lengthy battles over judicial philosophy. The interpretation of the law in terms of class-struggle, which was the battle-cry of the extreme Marxist School, has been replaced by a broader historical approach. Professor Trainin, who in the early 'thirties was bitterly attacked by the 'Pokrovski School' as being an upholder of 'classical, bourgeois, juridical philosophies', is to-day one of the leading exponents of Soviet law, and some of his recent writings have been translated as pamphlets for issue abroad with the approval of the Soviet authorities.

Against this background of the organs of security and the juridical system, the question is to what extent the Soviet citizen as he goes about his work and his play feels himself free and immune. There can be no doubt that he is more aware of, and more wary of, the police than the citizen of bourgeois countries. There, is, however, another aspect. If the Soviet citizen accepts the régime and is willing to co-operate with it, he is in no danger, and knows himself to be in no danger, provided he does not venture into political life. The Purge period ended six years ago. It struck deep into the consciousness of the people; and still affects their individual relations with foreigners. But the period, the 'black time', when they were afraid of each other has passed long since.

The weight of the security structure which rests on the shoulders of the nation is felt much more by the older age-groups of the population than by the young, who have experienced no other system and understand more easily how to move inside it without bumping into obstacles. The older age-groups remember either pre-revolutionary Russia, or the immense initial sense of freedom and opportunity which the Revolution brought to a large proportion of the people. The evidence of many observers regarding this sense of freedom is too detailed to be doubted. Some of this freedom has since been curtailed, for instance, by the labour law of 1940. But the general feeling of opportunity for the young in a country still starved of specialists in many professions is still apparent. The central Government developing Stalin's policy for the various nationalities of the Union has given freedom to the republics to maintain their own local cultures. This policy has widened the fields of opportunity open to the Uzbek, the Oirot, or the Armenian. The emergence of a system of increased rewards for hard work, the cultivation of sport and the arts, have to a large extent counterbalanced in the minds of the age-groups under forty any sense of curtailment of their freedom in a completely socialized State, to speak, to move about, or to worship.

These facts are not necessarily a defence of the internal passport; the restriction of movement so as to enclose certain cities and areas; the punitive taxation of the Church and of artel-industries; or to justify the single-party system; or the absorption of the State in its own security; or its control of published ideas and modes of art. In Russia, however, the Tsar has always moved with heavy boots. Awe, spiritual or temporal, is indigenous to such a religious people as the Russians. Much therefore is accepted as natural and understandable by them which to a foreigner would seem arbitrary or criminally casual. The Russian militiaman in his blue jacket and breeches, tall leather boots, peaked cap, large holster on hip, and a dogged expression, is usually the most obdurate, the perfect watchman or sentry. He represents and unquestioningly applies the regulations of an absolute power.

The Russia which has emerged from the war poses many problems. The main question-mark which hung over her strength and resources has been removed. Her régime has been proved stable. The Union did not disintegrate under pressure; and, on the whole, her people fought and laboured heroically. The incidental slackening of discipline and the desertions among the Russian occupation forces in Eastern Europe mean little; for Russians often decay when absent from the 'Rodyna-mat' (Motherland). For Soviet security this slackening of discipline outside the homeland matters little; and Stalin's Order of the Day of 23 February 1946, addressed to the Red Army, in any case already contained the warning: 'Successes in the training and education of troops are unthinkable without firm discipline and strict military order, the maintenance of which is the foremost duty of the entire army personnel.'

The returning soldier presents another problem. Incontestably many millions of men in the Red Army in war-time have enjoyed a freer life, with less 'paperasserie' and form-filling than surrounds their normal existence. Millions of Soviet citizens, either in the army or in the areas overrun by the Germans, or as prisoners of war or slave-workers, have had prolonged contact with the outer world. But it would be unrealistic to suggest that the returned warriors constitute any problem as regards Soviet security. They are far more likely simply to foster a wide demand for a lighter atmosphere and an easier life within the Soviet Union. Indeed Kalinin, late President of the Union, found occasion to mention, soon after the end of war, the tales of 'bourgeois comfort' brought back by demobilized Red Army men, and to remind a peasant-gathering that the Soviet system aims at social well-being rather than individual prosperity. Stalin in the Order quoted above exhorted the Red Army man 'not to boast of his services but to work conscientiously at his post'.

These two references to the attitude of the Red
Army man are further proof of the fact that the
Russians are by nature open of speech. Also, they
enjoy meetings, and are natural orators. The task
of the Soviet Government now must be inevitably
to inspire a tired people with the sense of elation
and drive which accompanied, however wisely or
foolishly, the first years of Revolution, and which
may again be vital to the immense task of reconstruction. On the evidence of a successful war one
would not suppose that the post-war phase presents
serious new problems to the Soviet Union after nearly
thirty years of the pursuit of security. Rather one
would surmise that the organs of security could
continue to acquire some stability and convention
of method.

PART III WORK

CHAPTER VII
INDUSTRY

WHEN Sir Stafford Cripps returned from Russia in 1942 the principal reflection which he made on the Soviet Union of that moment was its 'sense of urgency'. Many others who have lived in the Soviet Union would make the same observation, as it was applicable not only to the war period. In no branch of Russian life has this urgency been more apparent than in industry. Russia has been living her centuries in decades; and turning her civilization at the lathes. It is possible to question whether this urgency has produced steady, constant results. Another legitimate question is whether a quieter development might have achieved the same results. But such questions can be answered only on a mass of accurate data, and by specialists. The answers, in the manner of a specialist, would be of limited value.

In a brief examination of the Soviet way of life one can only note that towards one-third of the population now live by industry as against two-thirds who live by the land. Since 1917 all forms of industry have been fostered, with the possible exception of a few luxury trades. To take an extreme example, there are undoubtedly more precious stones being gathered and cut in the Soviet Union nowadays than in the Russia of 1913; but many of the stones are sold unmounted and not a great deal of jewellery is produced. In 1913 the

ratio of value of agricultural to industrial output
was about 60 : 40. By 1938 this ratio (at standard
prices taking account of the decline in the value of
the rouble) had been reversed. The change has by
now certainly proceeded farther. Professor S. N.
Prokopovicz, in his book *Russia's Economy under the
Soviets*, states with a great deal of argumentation:
'It is therefore to be concluded that the real growth
of gross industrial production in the post-revolutionary period is much nearer the index for the
growth of coal deliveries of 4·4, rather than the
figure 8·8 which is given to us in Soviet statistics.'
Even if we accept with Professor Prokopovicz that
that overall production of Soviet industry increased
by 4·4 times, there can be little conception in other
countries of the meaning of this great change for
the people of Russia.

Total mobilization of Britain for war from 1939
to 1945 wrought many changes in our economy; but
the inconveniences of the upheaval were minor
compared with the changes in the Soviet Union from
1917 onwards. Such surges in human experience
have to be placed in their contexts. This wave of
Russian experience has to be situated in a land of
great fields and rivers, where for centuries life had
been to a large extent controlled by the natural
seasons. In the past twenty-five years nearly
50,000,000 people left the land for the factories and
workshops and garages and have had to learn new
trades. A population equivalent to that of Britain
has needed to be taught new skills. At the same
time thousands of new foremen have had to be
supplied—and managers, cost-accountants, inspec-
tors, designers, and scientists. Beyond these it was

necessary to produce the myriad members of the learned professions who maintain such a population. The expanding output of the schools and universities, numbered in its hundred thousands, has not been able to keep up with the needs of the five-year plan; not only in providing all the necessary doctors and scientists, but also all the skilled labour which is required.

The 'urgency', or mobilization, of the Soviet Union in peace-time arose from the determination of the Communist Government to overtake the capitalist powers in their industrial potential within a brief period—a sad, frighteningly brief period. The population and the necessary material resources were already in existence. A reasonable amount of industry and a fund of skill in certain branches also existed. An exaggerated picture has been drawn of the industrial backwardness of Russia in the later Tsarist times. In fact, in the decade previous to 1913 the rate of industrial expansion was probably as high in Russia as in very few other countries of the world. The total capital investment by foreign countries in Russian enterprises would otherwise not have been so high as it was when the Revolution came; nor would the Intervention period have lasted so long. In addition to wheat, sugar refined in Russia was being supplied to more than a half of Europe, lumber had become an important trade, railways were rapidly spreading. The Tsarist arms output was large, even if not large enough, for the ensuing struggle with Germany and Austria-Hungary over a period of three years. Mining was developing in the Urals and the Donets Basin with foreign aid. Labour conditions in industry may have been appalling.

Nevertheless, since the Revolution was led by a 'politically conscious industrial proletariat', one should not ignore the industry which had produced those militant workers. Although not speaking specifically of industry, Stalin himself has written against accepting an exaggerated picture of Tsarist Russia as a 'centre of reaction'. The Communist magazine *Bolshevik* in May 1941 printed a letter stated to have been written by Stalin to the Politburo in 1934, in which he opposed a proposal to reprint in *Bolshevik* on the twentieth anniversary of the outbreak of the 1914–18 War, an article written by Engels in 1895. In this article Engels had analysed the world situation towards the end of the nineteenth century and explained on a Marxist basis the reasons why a world war was approaching. Stalin's letter of 1934 opposing the reprinting of Engels's article explained that Engels had, for reasons of German nationalism, painted an exaggerated picture of Russia as a centre of world reaction. He had done so, said Stalin, in such a way as to vilify Russia in the eyes of world opinion and especially of Great Britain.

Following the Revolution the era of reconstruction of industry with the aid of the New Economic Policy lasted until 1927. When the Government of Stalin decided to embark on 'building Socialism in our time', the Bolsheviks characteristically planned Russia's industrial advance according to a natural scheme of priorities. Electrification, investment in heavy industry, and some extension of internal communications were products of the First Five-Year Plan. In the Second, there was a further expansion of heavy industry and a great expansion

of processing industries. The interrupted Third
Five-Year Plan provided for an increase in light
industry and the consumption industries, and close
attention to the armaments and chemical industries.
Thus for thirteen years before the outbreak of war
the main industrial energies of the nation were spent
in preparation. Expansion towards a higher general
standard of well-being proceeded logically step by
step, according to artificial man-controlled laws and
not according to the 'natural laws' of supply and
demand of a capitalist society. The Soviet Union
was intended to be a plantation rather than a jungle.

A multiplicity of Commissariats dealing with
industry has arisen from State ownership, as I indicated earlier. The organization of these Commissariats has developed on a basis of trial and error.
The achievements in heavy industry, black metals,
non-ferrous metals, and the chemical industry have
been quantitatively outstanding. Production and
use of electric power has expanded rapidly, this
having been given special attention by the Communist Party since before the death of Lenin, who,
perhaps impressed by what he had seen in Switzer-
land, decided that electrification was a matter of
'first priority'. Equipment at the supply end is
uniformly good, and much of it is of foreign origin.
Standards of consumer equipment vary considerably.

There has in fact been a wide spread of light
industry throughout the Union, but its standards
are still uneven, being usually of average international
level for a small amount of production in any one
branch, and of 'utility' type for the remaining mass
of production. The textile industries, especially those
of Kalinin and Ivanovo, having a lengthy tradition

and a sufficient body of skilled labour as a nucleus at
the time of the Revolution, have greatly increased
their output and in some ranges such as printed
cottons have improved their quality and styles.
Men's suitings and women's woollen materials,
however, are in general still below Western standards,
being often light and poorly surfaced. Cotton goods
have naturally benefited by improvements in the
production of Central Asiatic cotton and the culture
of a number of long staples.

In these few years a vast amount of survey work
and prospecting has been carried out, with the result
that the whole range of mining throughout the
Union has been extended. This has been accompanied by what inside Russia are unquestionably
great technical advances. The achievements in
gasification of coal, and in developing new methods
of boring for oil, are considerable even by any
international standard.

In many industries there has been a tendency to
acclaim 'new victories' before a new method or
process has become a proven technique. This
tendency was, however, far more pronounced in the
early days of Russia's industrial revolution, and
claims are nowadays usually more conservative. A
recent assessment of American industrialists who
visited Russia in war-time would appear from their
published statements to be that output in an
American factory with similar equipment to that of
a Soviet factory would be nearly 50 per cent higher.
The verdict of some British factory experts has
been rather more favourable, probably because
by temperament they approach the question more
objectively.

To sum up it would be true to state that the most significant changes of an industrial character in Russia have been: the increase in consumption of power; the vast output of iron and steel; the success in certain highly skilled industries, such as those of aircraft and chemicals in keeping pace with the flow of technique in the outside world.

This immense variety of new industrial experience occurring throughout the entire Union and enduring over almost a generation, has been accompanied by squalid overcrowding in the existing towns and inadequate housing in the new cities. Had the Bolsheviks given themselves time to develop the country over fifty years instead of fifteen, some of the housing problems incidental to industrialization could have been mitigated. But for reasons of an extremely real foreign policy based on suspicion of 'capitalist encirclement', industry had to be condensed into five-year gestations. The resulting flow of people into the towns needed accommodation urgently, while at the same time the understandable desire of the revolutionary government was to deal with housing 'architecturally'. Town planning, development of sites, and attention to the architectural features of the new blocks of dwellings inevitably meant that new building was unable to keep pace with the influx of new town dwellers. The aimed-at average of floor space for each inhabitant of Moscow at the beginning of the 'forties was 90 sq. ft., but the actual average at that date used as a basis for allocating accommodation by the authorities was only 60 sq. ft. While it led to such inconveniences, in practice the planning system has proved itself from a national point of view. Only by the adherence of the authorities to a strict system of priorities, was it possible for the Union to possess the industry which supported the Red Army throughout the four years of war. It would be idle to deny, however, that the long spasm of effort by the nation took much from the vitality of the older people.

Professor Prokopovicz estimates that between 1928 and 1938 there was a total loss of 15,000,000 persons on the natural curve of increase of population indicated by the figures prior to 1928. He attributes much of this loss to famine conditions in the Ukraine and elsewhere in the early 'thirties. The loss which he estimates may be disputed; but there is no question that the First Five-Year Plan accompanied by the speedy collectivization of agriculture did severely hit the vital statistics of the Union. Millions of people were on the move, many families were separated, and the famine years killed several millions in the Ukraine, middle Volga region and the north Caucasus. In addition, throughout the 'thirties and on to the moment of the German attack there was no period in which the nation could take its ease. Industrial technique was being improved, and obligatory hours of labour were not lengthened until 1940, but the whole population was year after year constantly asked for more exertion, in new jobs and in new places. Results were apparent by 1939. From then until 1941 there was a visible improvement in the quantity of available goods and in their range and quality. The German onslaught had not lasted a year before that brief period of incipient comfort was being referred to as the 'good old days'.

The Soviet Russian way of life is lived by Russians. And as a race they have acquired in the past, habits of seasonal labour. Their very temperament is inclined to express itself in short waves of energy. Even their enthusiasm and warm-heartedness cannot always be sustained. The strenuousness of Soviet propaganda and its determined plucking upon that other cord in the Russian soul which is earnestness; both these features of the Party's activity can be traced to the need for creating in the Russian a more responsible and stable attitude to work. Millions of industrial workers have been asked to perform tasks for which they had little preparatory background, although this is not true of the newer recruits from the technical and occupational schools. The Government has endeavoured to rectify the widespread lack of industrial skill, but it is a fact that—to use a suitable metaphor—the column has had to proceed at the pace of the slowest vehicles. The Soviet industrial labour force, in general, is one which, not being disciplined in the normal manner of a capitalist society, requires in addition to a trade union *esprit de corps*, inspiration and encouragement from above. By all means possible to it the Government has sought the necessary managers and foremen and the methods of encouragement. In the early days of the régime politically conscious workers distinguished themselves and inspired others by individual feats of production. These were feats of individual endurance and skill as was implied by the name given to those who performed them, of 'udarniki' (shock-workers). Later the trail towards generally increased production was blazed by the Stakhanovites. Their method was and is to secure records by applying an improved technique to a particular type of work, with the record

E

of the individual usually dependent on the efforts of a small team. Gradually attention has been passing from the Stakhanovites to the creation of large numbers of 'brigades' or groups of workers who by team work secure a high and constant output. At the same time the system of piece-work rewards for the brigadiers and their teams has become more complicated. In the early days 'socialist emulation' was a propagandist phrase with a largely emotional value. Russians being Russians, the phrase translated itself even in the early days into competitions between factories of the same group. Nowadays the expression indicates a complicated system of rivalries between sections, shops, and factories, while the 'norms' of output for various skills are gradually raised, and the 'tysyachniki' (1,000 per centers), Stakhanovites, brigadiers, and section leaders earn piece-work bonuses.

The Soviet factory has been variously described. There are those who have acclaimed it as a marvel of technical development, spotless and filled with happy, singing workers. There are others who have exclaimed at what they termed its filth, its high percentage of discards, its spiritless workers, etc. To convey the reality is difficult. A factory is a factory anywhere, both dirty and productive, with bright shifts coming on and tired shifts going off. As usual, the Russians in creating their factories have tried to do everything at once—to create the lay-out and conditions of Bournville with resources not always adequate, and at the same time to put their main effort into obtaining a large output from an immense number of workers with as yet an insufficient number of superior personnel. In some factories there are rest-rooms and reading-rooms; but in all human societies the percentage of 'improvers' and socially minded people is small. The lay-out of the factories is often good, the equipment often first-class, especially when built to foreign models. But safety measures are alternately regarded with the utmost strictness and supreme laxity. In the factories I have seen there was the usual untidiness of Russian life, the lithe skill and drive of many of the women, the waste metal, the evident effort for improving technique, the inadequate repairs. In the grounds of some the original scaffolding lies rotting beside the foundations which have been laid for future expansion. Wall slogans abound, and boards with charts of the factory's progress, and banners for the leading brigades. There are canteens for all, and indeed these play an important part in the diet of the nation. The director's canteen will offer a better menu than that of the foreman and the foreman will often have a wider choice than the ordinary worker. The quality of the food is good in normal times. Many factories nowadays benefit by supplies direct from particular farms which are attached to them and which they frequently have to help with their own labour. Allotments are usually worked by individuals, but in some cases during the war, factories were made responsible for particular groups of allotments, and the whole system of allotments with State facilities in the distribution of seeds seems likely to continue well into the peace. Crèches are attached to most factories, and in the neighbourhood of important plants the workers' settlements are often well laid out in small blocks of flats with shrubs and trees. All in all, the effort put forward, sprawling and unequal though it is, seems a thousand times better than the life of the depressed labour in Tsarist factory tenements. As some of the latter still exist on the outskirts of Moscow and Leningrad, and owing to overcrowding have still to be used, it is still possible to form such a judgment.

From the days of the First Five-Year Plan onwards the authorities have been offering bonuses for ideas tending to greater efficiency in the plants or aiding new processes. Such ideas reach the machine of State originally through the works' production committees (which are not formed on exactly the same lines as British production committees). It is from 1942 onwards, however, that we have seen the real drive in Russia for increased individual output and team output. With millions of men mobilized in the forces and others engaged in ancillary work for the services, Russia for the first time experienced labour shortage. Hence in the later part of the war the campaign for improving technical methods, of saving time by improving assembly lines and by instituting here and there moving-belt systems. Standards of productivity of individual workers still vary enormously, and the method of obtaining improvement by 'good example', usually by skilled section leaders, is effective only where all the workers involved understand and are capable of applying the latest Soviet methods. Where in a factory a variety of skills is involved, precept and example need to be supplied to new labour by teacher foremen, and above them by junior administrators. Of these Russia has never had sufficient. One of the catchwords of the moment is in fact: 'During the war we created the lieutenants and the majors. Now we must have the lieutenants and majors of the factories.' Equally the task has been to secure a sufficient number of factory directors capable of taking initiative, of fulfilling plans, of resisting and not undertaking impossible plans, capable of accepting the great strains and the appropriate rewards, and able to resist the many temptations. The temptations derive both from the responsibilities of the director and from his opportunities. Sometimes he needs material in a hurry; sometimes he has it to spare. Thus from time to time a deal has been worked on the side in sand against scrap-metal or some similar exchange.

In spite of all the obstacles the skilled labour force has constantly risen and with it production. The large 'moving-belt' system, first applied at the Stalin automobile works in Moscow, has been put into operation in many other factories in the past three years despite the difficulties of doing this in wartime. The system of checking the accuracy of components, which was always an important aspect of Russian factories because of the low standards of the labour supply in the early years, has been revised during the war. Soviet experience has been the same as in war-time Britain, i.e. that checking at the earliest stages and so far as possible by the most automatic means, involves a saving of labour and a much smaller percentage of ultimate rejects.

One feature of the Soviet factory system, which may now be declining, is unevenness of production. Even in the factories, which in the late 'thirties were producing new records every few months, production was frequently not smooth and sustained. As Voznesenski, Malenkov and others have stated, output during any month might vary, e.g. for two-thirds of the month output might be below normal although the workers with Russian enthusiasm had vowed themselves to new feats, and in the remaining third, by overworking the machines and themselves, they would wind up the month ahead of their planned output. This involved in many factories greater wear and tear of equipment and personnel, higher overheads and a higher real cost of production. The Soviet Press has inveighed against such methods for years past, and it is therefore no carping criticism to record this matter of broken tempo. The fact is that a high sustained output is not natural to many Russians. On the other hand, the mass meeting, the passing of unanimous resolutions after a dozen people with a natural eloquence have said approximately the same thing, are genuine and spontaneous on many an occasion and lead to feats of work which would be surprising in any other country. It may be doubted, however, whether the additional day's work which is sometimes solemnly voted and performed in aid of a good cause, is quite so spontaneous. It is probably accepted as necessary inconveniences are accepted in other countries. Subscriptions to loans are also occasionally agreed and collected within the factories with a surprising unanimity. But the willingness of the Russian to take part in a collective decision is a fact grounded in history and not affected by any question of compulsion.

Soviet labour was at the outset considerably undisciplined. Much of the previous shiftlessness of labour was, however, eradicated by the Labour Law of 1940. Introduced at a time when the Finnish campaign and the war in Western Europe had caused a spurt in the already large armaments programme, this law tied labour down to the factories. The regulations were, in fact, similar in many ways to the British war-time rules for the direction and location of labour. Especially severe were the rules against lateness, slackness, etc. The basis of Soviet factory work had been the collective contract as opposed to the individual contract between employer and employee, which is still presumed to exist in England, as Sir Frank Tillyard has pointed out, in spite of the highly developed British system of trade union collective bargaining. The effect of the 1940 Labour Law was to remind the individual Soviet worker of his responsibility if he were to benefit by the general conditions of labour which had been collectively applied. Previously labour had been fluid. For the young, life was exciting. Jobs were plentiful. One could migrate between the farm and the factory. During the war special regulations going beyond the 1940 law and involving the establishment of a 'trudfront' (labour front) were introduced. Under these all adult labour could be directed as desired to seasonal emergency work. Women and children from the towns were in these war-time circumstances obliged to help in whatever way they could on the collective farms. Now in the first period of peace there has been a general easing of the war-time emergency regulations. As in other countries the mood of the people has been, 'Back to normal'. The Government was psychologically well advised not to order an immediate start on a new five-year plan, but to allow demobilization to proceed for some months before proclaiming a new effort.

In the whirl of Soviet development, of things new-made, new-broken, new-discovered and new-rejected, the trade unions have retained an important place. The State has demanded much of the available labour force, and the trade unions in a Socialist State have had to become national instruments. They have lost the internal political significance with which they were formed, since under the Soviet system the workers and peasants are by definition the holders of power. This presupposition has been carried to its logical conclusion, and the trade unions exist to smooth relations between the worker and the State. The task in fact involves them in much work which does not fall to British trade unions, such as responsibility for social welfare, various types of education, etc. The Soviet trade union still has a part to play in rate-fixing, since the unions are bound up with the economy of each factory. The Soviet factory possesses a works' committee, a Party committee, and a trade union committee, each factory having a single trade union except for certain special occupations. It would be difficult to assess how much of the old form of trade union feeling still exists, but it would be logical to suppose that it survives chiefly in such callings as are not organized in factories, such as the railways and mines.

As a result of the fact that membership of the factory's union is obligatory, the trade unions in most instances dispose of large funds, and have more power in bulk than might be apparent despite the fact that strikes do not occur.

Trud, the trade union newspaper, appears daily and has a large circulation. Its articles on foreign matters are often livelier than those of the Government organ *Izvestiya*, or the Party organ *Pravda*, and it possesses the advantage that its views are not official, and can be disavowed. *Gudok*, the railwayman's newspaper, is more specialized, but is also not without importance. As a further indication of the position which the trade unions hold within the framework of the Soviet system, it may be noted that the head of the All-Union Committee of Trade Unions, M. Shvernik, was elected in 1944 President of the Soviet of Nationalities, and in June 1946 succeeded the late M. Kalinin as President of the U.S.S.R.

It is still too early to define the ultimate position of the trade unions in Russia. Inasmuch as industry itself has been fluid throughout nearly twenty years, so also has the activity of the trade unions fluctuated. As recently as 1935 an entire Commissariat, that of Social Welfare, was dissolved and its work handed over to the trade unions. It is still too early to tell what further work might be given to them in the years of post-war reconstruction.

CHAPTER VIII
AGRICULTURE

JUST beyond the last block of new flats, standing self-consciously above the old wooden cottages, and just beyond the factory yard of the 'Kombinat', begins the countryside. Owing to the emphasis of the Soviet Press on the development of industry, and to an endless series of books about Russia's new age of steel and learning, the peasant background of Russian life is nowadays minimized. While peasant life may not be the same as it was twenty-five years ago, and though the country may be ruled by a Party which was originally the weapon of politically conscious factory workers—nevertheless the rural influences of Russia are still ultimately predominant. The total of the rural population is now practically the same as at the time of the Revolution (1 January 1917, 113·9 millions; 17 January 1939, 114·6 millions). The distribution nowadays varies considerably from that of Tsarist times. This is so partly because the area under cultivation has expanded, with an especially large increase in scientific or technical crops. Thousands of square miles of previously uncultivated or marginal land in all parts of the country—but more particularly in western Siberia and Central Asia—are now bearing crops as a result of new methods or better application of old ones.

A few foreign observers have preferred to concentrate on the rural life of Russia. Apart from the major studies of Sir John Maynard there is the series of books by Maurice Hindus, charged with emotion for the peasant, but also highly informative. Many facilities have been given to Sir John Russell and other agricultural scientists to study the development of Soviet agriculture. In fact the Russians have shown many of their collective farms to foreigners and have been more communicative in general about their agriculture than about almost any other branch of Soviet life with the exception of the theatre. Soviet agronomists have also exchanged ideas with foreign workers in the realm of agricultural experiment over the past twenty years. Altogether the mode of working of the collectives and a fair number of their results are known.

In examining other organs or branches of life in the Soviet State it has been right to consider primarily the impact of the institution upon the individual. In the case of Soviet agriculture it is probably more correct to discuss the influence of the peasant character upon the wishes of the Government. In the earliest years following the Revolution there were numerous experiments in a variety of districts in complete communalization of villages. Although local branches of the Communist Party took a sympathetic interest in such experiments, they received no organized support from the Government in the period of 'the land for the peasants'. Parcellation of the land was then the Government's policy in order, as Lenin wished, to retain the support of the peasantry for the Revolution. Only later was collectivization applied as a policy. In the first year of collectivization, 1929–30, the peasants and the local authorities in many districts were mistaken in their ideas of what it was that the Government desired. Was it a return to local village control through the 'mir' (the village community)? Or was it the formation of artels (companies) or of collectives, or of co-operatives, or of the most extensive primitive Communism? The pooling of livestock seemed to point in one direction, while the retention of the co-operatives seemed to point in another. Hence the turmoil in the countryside, well described by Sholokhov in *Virgin Soil Upturned*. Hence, also, the obstinacy of the peasants against co-operating wholeheartedly with the new system, which obstinacy extended far beyond the kulak class of richer peasants which was marked down for elimination. Resistance to the change in the basis of farming was strongest in the Ukraine, the north Caucasus, and Central Asia, and took the form principally of the withholding of grain and other produce from the market or from the Government's grain collectors. The former two areas are rich surplus-producing regions, and the last-named had not even the tradition of the village society which had long existed among the Great Russians. In the end, at the expense of a long battle of wills and many deaths through famine, the Government had its way. But it was obliged to allow private peasant farmsteads to continue where the owner wished, at the same time making it difficult in one way and another for them to prosper. Moreover, each collectivized farm worker was allowed to keep in the proximity of his cottage between five-eighths of an acre and two and a quarter acres of land. And throughout the later 'thirties and the 'forties, in all its dealings with the countryside, the Government through its myriad organs has still had to take account of the character of the peasant.

Superficially it might seem that the Karataev of *War and Peace*, who lived not so much a life as a part of a great living, was quite distinct from the mankind depicted by Solovyev, capable of and moving towards a transfiguration of his own species which would reflect and at the same time be fused with the Divine Logos. It might seem that both Russian examples of humanity had no part with the collectivized peasants of *Tikhi Don* or *Virgin Soil Upturned*. Actually one might say that Tolstoi, Solovyev, and Sholokhov were all accurate as observers, though their purposes differed. The peasant has become conscious to a greater extent than was Karataev; but he is still the peasant. Many writers have stated that he made the March Revolution of 1917 and the Bolsheviks of the towns made the Great October. From the outset the Bolsheviks disliked the peasants' solution of their troubles in the seizure of the land. But for a decade it went unchallenged. We shall see later what was the cost of the inevitable clash. Sir John Maynard summarized in *Russia in Flux* the historic attitude of the Russian peasant: 'All else, except the call of the land, has passed over the heads of this peasant people, as if it has been a dream. It is a people which the rigours of still unconquered nature and the cruelties of man have schooled into an infinite capacity for suffering: not into a love for it, as some fanciful interpreters have asked us to believe. Tolerant, pitiful, Christian in the spirit of the Sermon on the Mount, it has yet been capable of outbreaks of savage and horrifying violence, when the cup of

unconsciously accumulated rage was full. Certain
rudimentary social institutions it has made its own:
the family, the village commune, the working
partnership with chosen comrades. Beyond there it
has been non-political: and towards the institution
of the State, with one exception, it has been an-
archical, submitting only to the sense of helplessness
and to fear.'

The Revolution was the inevitable sequel, long
delayed, to the emancipation of the serfs in 1861,
though the subsequent form of the State was not of
the peasants' choosing. In the meantime, State
measures to aid the peasant had been inadequate,
and by the buying out of small holdings and their
regrouping, a class of prosperous farmers had been
formed who were further aided by the Revolution
and the N.E.P. period. When collectivization came
the poor and middle peasants were only too pleased
to break up the possessions of the kulak class. What
was more difficult for them to understand was that
they had to learn how to feed more than 50,000,000
people of the towns.

Soviet agriculture has seen as many changes as
Soviet industry—some even more fundamental.
Starting with the satisfaction of a land-thirst, proceeding through a long period of battle over possessions, Soviet agriculture had achieved an approach
to stability by 1941. That there was a certain
measure of stability is proved by its successful course
during the war. The war period saw further
changes; and the consolidation of others, such as
the strength of the collectives *vis-à-vis* the uncertain
economy of the towns. To explain the present
Soviet rural way of life involves tracing the history

of these changes. Firstly, we should note the increasing power of the kulaks during the N.E.P. period, and the rise of factors who dealt in the produce of the land. The Government which had to feed the millions streaming into industry from 1928 onwards was next obliged to collectivize farming, as it has since admitted. In one period of less than a year 50 per cent of Russian agriculture was collectivized—a breakneck procedure, which led to Stalin's encyclical *Dizzy with Success*. The period of agriculture wrecking followed, accompanied by the slaughter of millions of beasts. Next came the famine in the south and south-east; and later recovery at a rapid pace, leading to the bumper harvests of 1937 and 1938. Equipment within the collectives was modernized and a network of machine-tractor stations drawn over the country-side. Whereas in the first stages of collectivization many enormous State-run farms had been created, expensive of equipment and impossible to husband, a large number of these reverted in the middle 'thirties to village-run collectives. State working was retained only where such farms—of a reasonable size—could improve particular crops or strains of livestock.

As times improved the peasants in a peasant way began to devote too much time to their own plots, in order to sell their own produce in the free market. By the late 'thirties town goods were beginning to reach the villages as a result of the industrial Five-Year Plans. A new agricultural law was introduced determining the number of labour-days (the unit of calculation of the peasant's work) which must be performed by each member of the collective. By

1939 the total of livestock in the Soviet Union had recovered to the position of 1932 after the disastrous falling away caused by the struggle betweeen the countryside and the Government. After the recovery some 85 per cent of the livestock remained in the hands of the peasants.

In the meantime the collectives had begun to fit into the schemes of the Union's economic planning. New types of crop had become less unpopular as it was found that they brought more money. In the early days of the collectives the 'presidents' and 'secretaries' changed frequently, but by the beginning of the new decade their tenure had become longer. Local leaders emerged. The agronomist, the scientific agriculturist, who descended as a further tribulation upon the peasant's world, had begun to prove himself. In 1940 and 1941, following good harvests, the kolkhoz and sovhoz leaders were coming into the cities in the spring with much money in their pockets—to place new orders, to discuss programmes, and not to forget their wife's fur coat. A great antagonism still remains: but it is one of fact rather than of will. The towns are not yet sufficient suppliers of industrial and consumer goods to the countryside. Nevertheless, by 1941 the cottage of the Ukraine or of western Siberia showed signs of change, apart from its use of electric light. Even if one deducts a certain percentage of propaganda value, the Museum of Nationalities on the outskirts of Moscow reflects in its exhibits the violence of the changes which have occurred in the villages not only of the Moscow region, but also of Uzbekistan, etc.

With the war, the test for Soviet agriculture came.

The farmer left the cowshed and the tractor-driver
went off to man a tank. The question was whether
the State would still be able to obtain sufficient to
feed the workers of industry. By the agricultural
decree of 1942 higher norms of labour-days in the
year were imposed for collective farm workers. The
task was hard, especially for the women; but aided
by Lease-Lend supplies the State was able to obtain
sufficient food to maintain a limited system of staple
rations. The peasants throve in roubles by selling
their private produce on the free market. Goods,
for which they have a passionate desire, were difficult to obtain, but their rouble holdings mounted
into milliards. In the villages lies the invisible
inflation of the war era. Meanwhile the 1942 decree
still stands; complemented by the 1944 decree
regarding the restocking of the herds which had
been depleted in European Russia and especially in
the areas of German occupation. The local industries
decree of the same year was meant to complete the
picture by fostering local production of consumer
goods for the benefit of the countryside.

Russia's farmland once more at peace is mostly
collectivized. But it is important to note that the
collective farm is not an up-to-date version of the
ancient 'mir'. The purpose of the latter, which
existed sometimes surreptitiously, was to determine
in what manner the particular land of a village was
to be worked from year to year. The collective exists
as a form of rural factory, or productive mechanism,
which has a dual purpose. Firstly, it supplies a
planned part of the total national economy.
Secondly, it is intended to assist in raising the
cultural level of the peasants and transforming them

as a class into citizens of equal attainments with the
town workers, in the development of a 'classless
society'. The 'mir' was in many ways an obstacle to
rural progress; the collective, whatever the circumstances of its origin, has been a means of introducing
new standards.

Whether the peasant wishes it or not, he is
supplied with a library and a cinema. A small
laboratory is provided for the maintenance of clinical
standards in dealing with livestock and crops, and
an agronomist to plague the peasant with stories of
germs, blights, and soil diseases, which his fore-
fathers sensibly knew to be Acts of God. The
collective provides a school. It receives chemical
manures from the State. It has a director and a
secretary; it is continually expanding its activities—
wasting its time, as some of the peasants would
think, trying to grow good wheat on marginal land,
and butting its head against the obvious. New
crops of which Ivan had not even heard—rank weeds
some of them—have to be grown as part of a plan.
And still more strangely, the Government is willing
to pay for them.

Sixty per cent of what is grown disappears into
the maw of the State; and the collective has to keep
an accountant with an abacus, who sits on a stool
and shifts beads and yet is awarded at the end of
the year a formidable number of 'trudodni' (labour-
days). The collective introduces working in brigades,
and teaches new methods of sowing and reaping,
when everyone knows how to sow and to reap. The
collective buys machines instead of horses. Those
horses which it does buy it often obtains from a
State farm, where they are always trying to improve

the strains, instead of letting Ivan's horse breed on Trofim's mare. The collective often applies to the M.T.S. for tractors to do the ploughing or hauling, or for combines to harvest the wheat. In the spring the collective demands that all the machines be examined and repaired. In the winter it insists on education, and on work being done at home. It organizes meetings, and parties for the children; and gifts to the local towns. The M.T.S. people demand some of the crop for just a few days' work with their machines. The collective is certainly not an extension of the 'mir'.

A complete examination of the Soviet way of life in the countryside would demand that one should set down all the types of cultivation in the whole range of climates of the Union. It is perhaps more important to emphasize that the farming community is still subject to the Nature which it tends. In northern Russia the farming season, except at certain scientific stations, lasts five months. In the extreme south it lasts nine months. The hunting co-operatives of Siberia, though working within the same system, cannot be compared as a 'way of life' with a collective farm of the Velikie Luki region of which the staple crop is flax, nor with the sovkhoz of the Kursk province feeding its brood mares on the soft grass of the wooded steppe. All that can briefly be said is that the same scientific approach to agriculture by the régime is being applied at a swift pace in all regions. The Commissariat of Agriculture with an obligation to feed the 'dictatorship of the proletariat' is endeavouring to oust the precariousness from farming, which was a constant threat in the past. The great problem, especially in Asia, and

in parts of the Ukraine, has been to secure an
adequate water supply at all points. The second
problem has been that of expanding the sown area
into lands of insufficient chemical wealth or with an
over-cold subsoil.

Experimentation has in fact been at least as
developed in agriculture as in industry or in education. These experiments have ranged from the
vitally important to the trivial. They include efforts
to produce super-hardy cereals; artificial vernaliza-
tion of plants, which can then be flown in their
thousands to more northerly regions and thus make
use more quickly of the late northern spring;
experiments in concentrating artificially the soft
northern sunlight to secure quicker ripening;
artificial insemination which is already practised on
a large scale; efforts to produce naturally coloured
cottons, giant wheat, new types of bees; and many
tests with various soils and fertilizers. Not only
have tea, cotton, rubber, coffee, rice, fruits, and oil-
bearing seeds been grown on an expanding area—
but these crops have also been experimented upon.
Though from the scientific point of view the State
farms are the main centres of experimentation,
nevertheless many a relatively new crop or method
has been put to the collective farms to be fostered by
peasants with a limited background. The speed of
the system demanded this; but it is small wonder
that some of the Central Asiatic collectives staffed
by former nomads have proved haphazard in their
farming.

The stabilization, at least physically, of the
collectives is in fact a monument to the immense
will-power of the central government, if one takes

into account the planning programme enforced at
the same time upon the middle and lower peasantry.
Had the kulak class wished to co-operate with the
Soviet Government, it no doubt had the ability to
do so. But it was a profit-making class and not one
which would necessarily submit to dictation regarding its cropping rota, such as was inherent in a fully
planned economy. Nevertheless, the disappearance
of the kulak farmsteads, which frequently contained
the best land in any district, necessarily caused an
original set-back in the production of certain regions.
This was particularly so in the surplus-producing
areas which had traditional staple crops; such as the
wheat and beet of the Ukraine, the wheat and fruit
of the mid-Volga and the North Caucasus. The task
of recovering production had to be given to the
former poor and middle peasants. The actual
recovery achieved, whatever the arguable figures, is
a further tribute to the adaptability of the peasantry
themselves. Much, no doubt, is also due to the tight-
ness of the direction supplied by the frequently
changing kolkhoz leaders. In the meantime the
village has lost its calm. The girls on Sundays wear
printed frocks, the men have abandoned their birch-
bark shoes for leather boots. The village has produced Marshals, doctors, scientists, tractor-drivers,
and diplomats. It has acquired electric light, oil
stoves, oiled cloth, and often motor transport.

In this transition many groups of villages have
undoubtedly been aided by the existence of a near-by
sovkhoz or State farm. In some ways a guinea-pig,
the State farm has been the institution which has
taken the shock of experiments in scientific farming, and passed on its acquired knowledge to the

collective farms. In the first place, from 1928 onwards, enormous holdings of up to 800 square miles
were grouped into single undertakings. The intention
was that with a lavish mechanical equipment they
should demonstrate how the State could win an
enormous yield from the soil. In the early 'thirties
Trust Farms of similar size were formed to produce
livestock. Plans, however, ran ahead of results.
For example, in Russia the second weeding of the
corn is vital to the crop, but in such huge undertakings as the early State farms the available labour
force was often insufficient for the task. Quickly
learning from its mistakes, the State adapted many
of the sovkhozes to reasonable size and more limited
purposes. They became model farms of intensive
cultivation, sources of new strains of draught
animals, sources of skilled personnel. Farmers
trained in the State farms, could move on to the
collectives and give them a more stable leadership
than had been the case in the early years when large
numbers of collective-farm directors were supplied
out of the towns with an inadequate knowledge of
the hazards of farming.

By now it is possible to talk of a Soviet way of life
in the countryside. The system of co-operatives and
artels has existed for over twenty years and the
larger system of collective and State farms for more
than fifteen years. The number of private farmers
has dwindled to only some six per cent of rural
households. The collective farmer has his own plot
and takes his part in the collective. Old bitternesses
remain among the higher age groups. The peasant
everywhere worships as before the possession of
solid objects. He sees the State take much of the

collective produce, at a fixed price. He is still suspicious, like the peasant of other lands, of revealing all that he possesses. To some extent he has adopted the materialist attitude of the State towards the soil and towards his livestock. The money which the collective earns has a share for him and his family. He can sell the produce of his own plot as he pleases. Thus where a large family has accumulated earnings of a period of years it is not surprising that during the war the head of the family should have come forward and presented a million roubles to a loan, or purchased an aeroplane for the State.

Compulsory schooling, the wireless, the cinema and much shifting among the population has altered the outlook of many inhabitants of the villages. What was formerly an unreal emotional yearning for the life of the town has in the past twenty years been put into practice. The peasant boy with a head for figures becomes a book-keeper.

The early years of the régime have passed, when many went into the villages from the towns to escape the rigours of Revolution and famine. In those earlier years there was also much roving by the peasant population. The man of the Don wandered to the foothills of the Urals and back. He had a sense of a continent in which to roam, and jobs were easy to obtain without special skills. Now, however, the countryside is much more settled, despite the upheaval of the war and the migration of some thirty millions from the west, eastward.

In a thousand ways the village is nearer to the town than ever before. Life in the town begins to set the fashion for the village. Furthermore, the village is less self-sufficient. The needs of defence

and of heavy industry having been placed before
those of light industry, and the local industries
which were the strength of the countryside having
declined enormously, the village is still under-
equipped. It has been seized up in a larger economy
and the wants of that system have to some extent
become its own wants. Against this it is fair to say
that the village is potentially rich. Whatever price
the State wishes to pay for the produce of the land,
the State has to come to the village and bargain.
Even if the prices are fixed elsewhere, the effect is
the same. Actually, the State buys at a medium
price and sells much of the food crop to the town
consumer with a heavy subsidy. Similarly, the
products of industry are bought at a 'costs-plus'
price and sold throughout the countryside where
necessary under subsidy. The State, incidentally,
recoups its losses through the sales-tax in other
directions.

In the relations between town and country lies
one of the most important future aspects of the
Soviet way of life. The gulf which existed in some
of the Western countries between the town and the
countryside as a result of an early industrialization,
is not likely to be so wide in Russia. One possibility
—even a probability—of the next decades is that a
proportion of industry will come into the Russian
countryside. And if the past decade has shown any-
thing, it is that even when he is not quite capable of
understanding it or of maintaining it, the peasant
has no fear of the machine. Like all Russians, he
adores gadgets.

CHAPTER IX

DISTRIBUTION AND CONSUMPTION

IN a Socialist economy, distribution is likely to be more artificial than its counterpart in a capitalist society where distribution tends to flow along the channels of demand. This truism has been amply demonstrated in the Soviet Union; which has had to work out its system of distribution and consumption from the starting-point immediately after the Revolution at which production was minimal. Nationalized methods of distribution began with the Revolution—Lenin being obliged to take this step with regard to wheat and bread as early as 1918. But throughout the N.E.P. period until 1928 collective methods of distribution were not pressed forward with rigid enthusiasm. Distribution tending in any developed economy to be essentially a middleman's task, N.E.P. offered scope to private distributors. For this reason much of the Soviet State's distributing mechanism has been evolved since 1927. The policy of the State towards the co-operatives and the smaller artels (light industrial or trading companies) has been stabilized during the period of the Five-Year Plans. While a larger proportion of distribution has been carried out by these means, the system has also expanded in more recent years of distributing selectively some of the State's products through the factories and the collective farms.

Planned consumption at planned prices proved extremely difficult to organize smoothly in the early 'thirties. It was only with the growth of administrative experience of the relevant Commissariats in planning that the process became regular. Over the past eighteen years there have been numerous changes in the Soviet policy of distribution. For instance, there was the question whether to institute large chains of shops selling a wide range of goods or whether to have a large number of small concerns selling the products of particular State trusts or factories. Another question was whether distribution should be carried out on an all-Union or republican scale and how it should be financed. Equally, a policy had to emerge regarding the different types of shop, and whether these shops should or should not stimulate the sales value of their articles. Finally, it was necessary to decide how to distribute effectively so as to cover gaps in supply —gaps both quantitative and qualitative.

As the system now stands, Commissariats exist to determine and foster the production of light goods, leather goods, textiles, food, fish, and canned goods. The actual mode of operation is chiefly through production trusts and retail trusts. Distribution is also effected through a large number of co-operatives and through various artels which are usually at the same time both production and retail units. Furthermore, the Commissariat for Foreign Trade, through its trade representatives abroad, has brought back many ideas which have influenced Soviet policies in distribution and consumption.

There are several forms of co-operatives in the U.S.S.R., such as those of the consumers, agricultural and handicraft producers, and the last-named includes the organizations of fishermen, hunters, and invalid workers. The consumers' societies, which are divided into groups representing town workers, agricultural workers, railroad and water transport workers, form the largest section of the co-operatives. In 1930 a greater measure of State control was introduced and the consumers' co-operatives were reorganized with a view to 'streamlining' this section of the distribution system by doing away with all unnecessary branches. The societies were organized on a regional basis and the regions instituted a system of control of the stores, shops, bakeries, etc. The number of consumers' societies, urban and rural, which in 1927 had totalled 28,609, was reduced by 1932 to 3,629. But throughout this period of change the volume of trade of the consumers' societies remained over half that of all the co-operatives. At the same time the trade of all the co-operatives combined was about twice that of State trade.

Whatever achievements have been made in Russia in distribution and consumption since the Revolution have been gained under the spur of the general economic situation. The Soviet Government has made an attempt, an enthusiastic and even ruthless attempt, to create a new standard of civilization for more than 170,000,000 people. New social needs have been established, accompanied by an assumption that there will be certain minimum standards for each individual. This attempt, in a society of under-consumption, has meant that a great 'stretch' or pressure was put upon the distributive trades. Short of instituting a rationing system for all products and consumption goods, the problem was how to distribute widely, if not entirely fairly,

the limited goods available. Hence the inevitable
importance of the co-operatives, and of the factories
and collective farms as channels of trade.

It would not be too difficult to make a detailed if
somewhat sorry analysis of Soviet distribution from
a purely dialectical standpoint. It could be shown
how methods have been caused by purely material
needs, and how quantitative progress in production
has led to sudden qualitative changes. Such an
examination, however, would tend to ignore the
psychological factor which is known to be of extreme
importance in matters of distribution and consumption. For example, it would ignore the fact
that when I visited a collective farm and dined in a
cottager's home, it was not the exquisitely prepared
chicken which I was expected to admire but the dish
of pear-drops and other boiled sweets on the table,
brought from the neighbouring town as a symbol of
factory-produced luxury.

In the Soviet Union demand has always exceeded
supply. Nevertheless, the State has deliberately
modified its system of general distribution in recent
years in order to put forward a 'shop-window' of
certain demonstratively luxury trades. These include
some of the restaurants at health resorts, the ice-
cream shops, art shops, the saloons of the cosmetic
trust 'Tezhe', certain of the hair-dressers, etc. All
these reflect the determination of the ruling Party to
create a society with standards of culture to which
the individual can aspire. In Russia the shop has a
civilizing function and the 'Atelye' (women's dress-
makers), the 'Mekha' (furriers) and the hair-dressers
are intended to aid the Soviet system. Similarly, the
dietetic food-shops and the furniture specialists.

Efforts, of course, have been made to meet demand. But this has not been easy because although there has been a constant demand, it has come from a people incessantly shifting, in a society undergoing catastrophic changes. In various republics, populations have bulged here and wilted there. To meet this demand in a lengthy period of emergency, supply has been organized as during the war, tanks and aircraft were organized. For any consumption article other than food to be authorized for production within the term of Soviet planning, it must constitute a certain obvious need or 'priority'. Thus articles are planned and produced in bulk; but not necessarily simultaneously and in a continuous flow. Hair-pins may flood the market, or red hats, or swan-down berets, or beige glacé shoes. But hair-nets, red hand-bags, white scarves, and beige gloves may not reach the stores at the same time to enable the Soviet woman easily to equip herself with all accessories. Equally, large loads of champagne may reach the towns of Central Siberia at a time when valenki are scarce. This is not a captious criticism, since these irregularities may be incidental to any society of under-consumption and may be the result of unavoidable economy in transport. It is a fact that the range of goods broadened from 1939 until the outbreak of war in Russia, especially in textiles and electrical equipment, while the quality of all paper goods improved considerably. Department stores increased in numbers. The lines of goods were still limited, giving a somewhat monotonous appearance to the shops, but distribution was becoming smoother.

The standards of public utilities (electricity, gas,

telephones, etc.) have not only risen, but what is interesting in addition, is the amount of experimentation from the consumer's point of view. Rapid increase in the use of electricity in the Union is common-place knowledge, but it should be borne in mind that it will, nevertheless, take another decade before all the villages are supplied. What is surprising is that one does meet electric power at a vast number of points—with all the attendant services such as telephones, public loud-speakers, electric irons (often of poor quality), and in some towns, electric bakehouses. Gas is supplied in all towns of any size, and in some, such as Kuibyshev, the hot water from the gas-works is used for central heating of houses in parts of the city. Natural gas from the oil-fields below the Urals has also been piped across hundreds of miles to provide light and fuel for towns in the southeast of European Russia. Municipal water supply, provided in all large towns, is a more serious problem throughout most of the Union, either owing to scarcity of water or its inaccessibility. Before the war the supply of fuel was not a serious problem, and much of the distribution was done by the municipalities. A large proportion of the radio-listening is done to loud-speakers wired to the communal network in the towns and the radio has come to be accepted as an inevitable communal service.

Of the services mentioned there is a heavy consumption. The Russian uses what is to hand. He is generous when dealing with his own people; and at the same time he is a large consumer—of life, of himself, of everything. The public services, moreover, are cheap, and as not only the Russian but also his wife works, the two find that utilities do not form a large part of their budget.

The Russian is also a heavy consumer of transport facilities. Trains, buses, trams, taxis; some are good, such as the electric trains, the Moscow buses; but others are bad. Some of the furious energy of the Soviet era has, however, gone into development of the means of travel. Transport ranges from the Moscow Metro to the horse-drawn sleighs of the provinces driven by the immemorial 'izvozchiki'; from the trolley-buses of Moscow and Leningrad to the reeking third-class railways coaches crammed with peasants and their bundles and the opaque blue smoke of 'makhorka'. I do not remember having seen in Russia a public conveyance which was not crowded; except an occasional Moscow tram on a weekday afternoon. The number of conveyances may still be insufficient; but one is tempted to believe that the more conveyances there were the more would Russians travel. They delight in movement, and the crowded tram is probably a fair symbol of Russia.

The social services should also be considered under the heading of consumption, because they have been sufficiently stabilized to be now part of the way of life. The working of the health and pensions services, for instance, is in detail probably as uneven as most features of life in this rapidly changing society. But the tendency is towards their becoming part of the system of distribution. The Soviet claim is that State expenditure on social and cultural services for the working people constitutes a considerable additional source of income to the average family. In 1938, this addition was estimated by the State at thirty-six per cent. The State was paying eighty per cent of all cultural expenditure and over ninety per cent of all health costs.

The social insurance services are controlled and administered by the trade unions. They pay out sickness benefits, maternity benefits, pensions to temporary invalids, and funeral benefits. They provide rest homes, sanatoria and holiday resorts, organize Pioneer camps and workers' sporting activities. The health services have been expanded rapidly to cover an immense territory in which extremes of climate and endemic disease such as typhus or tuberculosis historically claim many victims. The need for doctors and nurses is still immense; especially of the latter, since many women have been attracted by the opportunities to qualify as practitioners, who would otherwise have become professional nurses and raised the standards of that vocation. Although there are large numbers of young doctors and new hospitals, the health services are still concerned more with curing than preventing. It would be unfair, however, not to point out that where these services have had a prophylactic opportunity such as in the treatment of maternity cases, the maintenance of health centres, crèches, etc., the results have been steadily apparent. Even during the war the children of Russia had a bonny appearance in a great many cases—and the principal local causes of any decline were malnutrition or typhus. Sanatoria and rest-homes, often architecturally well-adapted to their surroundings, were built in large numbers at Black Sea coast resorts and in the Crimea, in the middle Volga region and the Urals during the twenty years after 1921. These were in some cases for the diseased, and in others for holiday purposes. In addition to enabling a reduction in the incidence of tuberculosis, they also to some extent allowed of an economy in the services of the doctors available to the Soviet Union. Additional medical services are also available to the nation through the fact that doctors are allowed to practise privately, outside their hours devoted to State institutions. The Russian tradition is that the patient on leaving after a consultation presses what fee he can afford into the palm of the doctor on shaking hands, or leaves a sum in an envelope. Such tradition has its disadvantages as well as advantages. It is also natural, perhaps, that the Party member, as one of those actively supporting the mechanism of the State, is usually able to obtain more easily the benefits of specialized medical attention. During the war, the experience of the Commissariat of Health was in many ways similar to that of its counterpart in Britain. The national system of health protection which had been largely built up since the Revolution, was able to meet the problem of contagion, although it naturally could not prevent a high rate of malnutrition in many towns and some rural areas. Children's diseases were even reduced, and outbreaks of typhus were dealt with by special 'flying squads' which isolated epidemic areas. The tuberculosis rate rose, on the other hand, owing to the loss of many sanatoria and the strains of war.

Libraries, now speckled through the Union, may also be regarded as a feature of the Socialist system of distribution and consumption. As they are attached to large numbers of scientific and industrial institutions and factories, as well as existing as separate public libraries, they are responsible for the

F

distribution of much of the reading matter within
the Union. The number and range of books available
has grown year by year. Even in a small collective
farm some of the volumes in a tiny library will be
well thumbed—probably novels and poetry and not
necessarily the volumes of Herzen, Marx, and
Turgenev demonstratively brought forward by the
young librarian well aware of the responsibility of
being visited by foreigners.

The still under-developed system of Soviet distribution and consumption is now returning to normal
after the war period of strain and partial break-
down. During that period a great proportion of the
resources of the system were diverted to the services.
The overall reduction in civilian consumption goods
at the middle of the war period was probably as high
as forty per cent, which in the circumstances of
Russia was very close to the maximum possible if the
efficient continuance of a large economy were to be
assured. The ration scales introduced for the civilian
population were graded according to the work
performed by the citizens, viz., heavy workers,
sedentary workers, dependants. Apart from staple
rations, consumption goods of the scarcer type such
as cigarettes and vodka went largely into privileged
channels. The factories and collectives became the
main distributing agencies for many of the types of
article still available, such as rubber boots, valenki,
padded clothing, etc. At the same time the free
market, which had previously existed on a small
scale only, being a less dependable and more
primitive form of distribution, acquired a new
importance. Many citizens sold some of their
possessions through the commission shops and with

the roubles bought extra food from the peasants in the market. The extreme scarcity of goods on the free market automatically involved inflation prices, since the Government had set its face against any wide system of barter. The same tendency was aided by high piece-work earnings and by all the incidental financing of the services—requisition chits, soldiers' pay, etc.

The first move towards pulling the system back to normal was the institution of 'commercial shops' which by charging high prices have pulled some of the inflation currency back into the hands of the administration. Prices in these and in the normal shops have recently been reduced and in February 1946 Stalin was able to announce that rationing would shortly end. Complete control of the legal means of distribution has enabled the Soviet Government to permit the 'free market' as a kind of useful safety-valve. It is true, of course, that not only the 'free market' falls outside the scope of official distribution. In addition, innumerable other transactions take place ranging from the almost legal to plain corruption. At their best, these transactions are 'okaziya' or opportunities incidental to any system. Usually, however, they constitute what is termed 'blat'. The theatre ticket which reaches you instead of its rightful destinee is obtained 'po blatu' at a slightly increased cost. Until human beings have developed a higher automatic respect for the rights of others and of the community, 'blat' exists. The chances of indulging in 'blat' are, however, very limited for the main mass of little factory workers and farmers. Distribution to them normally comes through the co-operatives and consumers' societies,

with the State subsidizing much of what they
purchase.

Much is known concerning Soviet prices and they
have been discussed in detail in a number of books,
notably by Leonard Hubbard, and Alexander
Baykov, but the extent of State subsidizing in the
processes of obtaining and handing on of materials
and products is not completely known. Similarly,
the total percentage of waste is also difficult to
assess. In the post-Revolutionary era of great
expansion and of capital investment, a high percentage of the activities of the State have had to be
carried out on the basis of credit. The products of
these many operations have, therefore, required
subsidy to enable them to pass on into other sections
of the national economy without involving pro-
hibitive and ever-rising costs. That the Soviet
Government is anxious to end this period in which
the State is the great loser, is shown by the insistence
of Soviet economists in recent years on the importance of cost-accounting. Individual State enterprises are being increasingly required to reach and
maintain themselves at a 'costs-plus' stage which
would provide for their own future investment
needs. To attain this level a higher productivity
of labour and improvements in technical method
are constantly necessary—and with both these
advances must be linked higher efficiency in distribution.

Much consumption remains and is likely to remain
within the sphere of subsidized operations, e.g. food,
utilities, public conveyances and communications of
all kinds, books, etc. This subsidizing of prices has,
of course, an anti-inflationary action, as the British

Government demonstrated when it adopted a similar tactic for food during the Second World War. One constant aim of the Soviet Government has been to maintain as high an internal value for the rouble as possible, and to set a gold value upon the rouble for external purposes, largely as a measure of security. A wide gap exists between the average consumption value of the rouble at home and its international exchange rate. In terms of newspapers the rouble is worth 7*d*., in terms of white bread 2*d*., but in terms of books its value may be as high as 1*s*. 6*d*. It has been possible for the Soviet Government to insist on this discrepancy over many years partly because the Union is a large gold producer, but also because the State has complete control of the means of production and of the goods and services produced. Russia normally regulates her foreign trade according to her policy wishes—and over the years has varied her tactics from plain 'dumping' to the hardest bargaining in the gold market. To allow for this trade and for the needs of defence, all the more necessary has she found it to regulate internal distribution into those channels considered to have priority. This is one of the main reasons for the amount of retail trade conducted through the factories and the collective farms.

Much consumption trade, e.g. shoe-repairing, garages, wooden articles, is best conducted through small organizations. In Russia this is provided for by a system of small artels, or groups of small workshops in any one town or district. These groups are co-operatively conducted as regards purchase of raw materials, maintenance of prices, and standards of work. But they are severely limited in their powers as employers of labour; and apart from the percentage of their income which is supposed to be retained in the artel for upkeep and capital development, they are heavily taxed. For the production of women's clothes and styles there exists also a network of 'atelye' (dress-makers). It has been the function of these shops gradually to introduce a better standard of clothes and of fashions, and to put before the Soviet woman the trends of style which have been tested at the shows of the 'Dom Modeli' (Central Models Shop).

Unquestionably, for the development of a variegated surface to life in the Soviet Union, much remains to be done to expand this type of distribution. The advent of a socialized system and the movement of many millions of people to new centres and new employments destroyed a great deal of the local industry and cottage industry of Russia, which had been one of the strengths of the country. The Soviet Government showed its awareness of this gap in passing a decree in 1944 which was intended to provide for an immense recrudescence of local industries. The decree came in war-time—when even locally raw materials were difficult to obtain, and trained personnel was still scarcer. Moreover, handicraft skills, once lost, are not easy to regain. For a dozen years security for the worker had lain in taking one's skill inside a factory. The position of the individual in the N.E.P. period and the early Planning years had been reversed—and to revert once more to local industries is proving difficult for the man who has become accustomed to industrial piece-work rates.

Meanwhile, in the past fifteen years the standards

of the Soviet products in circulation and the methods of distribution have been improved. It is fair to say that a considerable part of this improvement is due to imitation of American and British methods. The styles, the practicality of goods, the methods of packing and of canning were rising rapidly during the years 1938–41. The product frequently lacked the superficial finish of the Japanese imitation of Western goods; but in contrast it usually displayed imagination and the 'unsound' article was becoming steadily rarer. The 'Zis' motor-car, despite its low-slung rear and its undistinguished weight-power ratio, was already a useful car and not too 'ladylike' for Russian conditions. She took her fences well. The People's car which was beginning to come on to the market at about 9,000 roubles in 1941, bore strong signs of Opel paternity; but was likely to prove a definite achievement and was no more cramped than many a small British car. At the same time style and attractiveness was beginning to enter into many an article—particularly food products, cosmetics, small household articles, sweet-stuffs, tobaccos and cigarettes. Window-dressing is still essentially un-Russian; though here and there in the larger cities a beginning has been made against the native tendency to put a little of everything into the shop windows. The most marked achievement in this line was made in the food shops in the late 'thirties, which displayed dummy cheeses, hams, fish, etc., made with considerable realism and definitely contributing to the brightness of the streets, even when times were hard. Harmonicas, accordions, pianos, and stylish radio-sets mainly after German and Polish models, were in the shops in quantity before the German attack. Latvian velours and felts were making a welcome addition to the styles of women's hats. Reasonable red wine sold at 12 roubles (about 2*s*. 6*d*.) and a sweet champagne at 18.50 roubles (nearly 4*s*.).

Stalin had said in 1933, to the immense relief of the average worker: 'Life has begun to show more happiness, more brightness.' Not until some years later did the little luxuries begin to appear in quantity and in the manner which gradually converts luxuries into accepted standards. One of the major effects of the war, and by all human standards one of its meanest crimes, is that it tore away this incipient pleasantness crowning the bitterness of Soviet effort as if the bride's garland were suddenly removed from the head of a hard-working young Ukrainian girl.

Despite improvements in the 'thirties, despite the lessons of the war, Soviet distribution is still not regular. The economy after the war is necessarily one of scarcity. Nevertheless, many articles, even luxury goods, have begun to reappear in the shops, and psychologically the atmosphere is thereby much lighter in spite of the size of the task of reconstruction. To the younger citizen the problem is perhaps mainly a question of rebuilding to a standard not far above that of 1941. A vast majority of the population knows only the Soviet way of life and how to move within it, taking its advantages, avoiding where possible its severities. The older age-groups, especially those of the former 'middle classes', remember nostalgically the profligacy of some sides of Tsarist Russian life. For them Soviet life is still complex in a way which it is not to the young factory-girl. She has grown up within her surroundings. Their harshnesses appear to her inevitable, their pleasures very real. Soviet distribution and consumption is not by any means egalitarian—and it provides few opportunities for the embryo of wastrel and spendthrift which lies embedded in every Russian. Those luxuries which are available mean therefore more to him than the foreigner can comprehend. Hence the excitement of the young girls at the Bolshoi Theatre, calling back the ballerinas a dozen times or more. Hence in a different way the men in the queues for eau-de-Cologne during the worst period of the war; I have seen them drink it and reel in the street. Naturally, they were only an outcrop on the face of the people; but they were Russians.

PART IV THE PRODUCT

CHAPTER X

MAINTENANCE

THE fruits of the Spirit are, according to the English:
love, joy, peace, long-suffering, gentleness, goodness,
faith, meekness, and temperance. In making this
examination of the Soviet way of life it is not
compulsory that one should attempt to pass judgment on the extent to which it may produce the
fruits of the Spirit or fulfil either the Law of the
Gospels or Canon Law. What is self-evident, however, is that a completely socialized way of life
demands certain attributes from those who lead that
life. There is no catechism, no fundamental text
to which one can refer in the case of the Soviet
Union. But the Soviet system in practice does
demand from and endeavour to inculcate in its
followers a number of qualities or attributes which
in the common experience of humanity are hard to
acquire, *inter alia* patience, enthusiasm, discretion,
devotion, attentiveness, and a desire to improve.
If these qualities are not sufficiently developed in a
large enough number of citizens, the system will
inevitably undergo serious strain or dislocation. But
to preserve these qualities, once the emotive flush of
Revolution had passed, required a developed scheme
of propaganda, example, and maintenance. Within
this scheme established by the Soviet State can be
included the educational organs of all types; the
Press and publicity machinery; and the Church in

its newly recognized functions. This is not to deny
that these functions or organizations have a value
'an und fuer sich' in the Soviet Union. But they
must also be regarded as bricks in the Soviet
edifice.

The Soviet Government and the ruling Party have
in fact worked out an elaborate maintenance system
to back their particular economy and mode of life.
Exhortation of a blatant or more subtly formative
character meets the citizen throughout most of his
waking hours. The many millions of peasants and
unlettered townspeople in Russia and in Asia who
convulsively rid themselves of their former controls
between 1917 and 1921, were due material for a vast
social experiment. They had ability, enthusiasm, and
need. The immediate slogans placed before them
were such as to appeal to the latent idealism of all
races. But in fact the experiment of modernizing
and socializing at the same time, was one which
called for a large number of thinkers, scientists,
architects, doctors, etc.—as well as professional
soldiers. The régime had rapidly to become didactic.

In the early stages of the régime, education was
treated as a new right which had been acquired by
the populace. The Party at an early date, however,
took the view that education was a duty, and was
not above using considerable moral pressure to reduce
illiteracy; with results which are impressive in
number if unequal in quality. In Central Asia
women were even forced to meetings and classes
at the pistol point—a proceeding which is understandable only if one conceives the hatred which the
local menfolk had of feminine enlightenment. Looking back over twenty years to the early revolutionary

period with its Islamic fervour for proselytism, it is difficult to recapture the atmosphere of those times. The accent was all on theory and on experimentation. Of necessity it has later been placed on maintenance of the Union through the production of a wide range of specialized types. The educational system at present in use is thus the outcome of much experience. It is in this light that the recent changes ending co-education in middle schools and enforcing a stricter discipline are regarded by the Russian. They are, so far as he is concerned, not retrogressions to a more conservative form of education. Since 1917 his country has tried and assessed all the 'advanced' methods of the outside world. They have been examined, their results weighed. Perhaps some of the methods have been tried in circumstances and with material resources which condemned them in advance to failure.

The Second World War was a major test for the Soviet system of education for which so much had been claimed. Early in 1942, the Soviet President, M. Kalinin, commented: 'We gave our best to our youth. The question was whether they would prove soft. But Soviet youth has justified our trust.' The characteristic qualities of Russian troops had in the meantime been displayed by Soviet youth—fortitude, courage, and loyalty. But this did not by any means imply that the educational standards of the nation were satisfactory for the long gruelling test of a modern scientific war. In 1943 changes were introduced throughout the system of education with a view to consolidating the experience gained. The accent henceforth was to be on basic discipline, and a series of rules of courtesy were to be observed by all scholars. Punishment was allowed where necessary. Boys and girls were to be separated during the years of adolescence. Their curricula were to vary. The aim was to be the production of bread-winners and fighters, and mothers. Already in the late 'thirties changes had been effected in the system of higher education so as to limit free entrants. Except in the cases of those who had obtained 'excellent' marks in all subjects, students would have to pay some forty per cent of their expenses. The number of 'stipends' or bursaries was cut down. Inevitably, it became less easy for the provincial peasant's sons to enter a university. On both these occasions of major change the public explanation was not that the system had previously been wrong, or that there was 'a return to tradition', but that the Government was improving the scheme for the development of cultured Soviet citizens.

An atmosphere of educational effort permeates Russia to-day. While it is true that the first wave of enthusiasm for bringing basic knowledge to the older age groups in the villages and farms has passed with the years, the main organized effort in education continues. In all the towns and many villages, crèches and nursery schools exist with years of experience, to give some millions of children early practice in organized games and healthy habits. The parents of those who are able to make use of one of these institutions pay according to their means. The 'detski sad' (kindergarten) with its child-size furniture, its garden, and its portraits of Lenin, Stalin, and other leaders, its tiny cots for afternoon sleep, has produced millions of children with a smile, a healthy pair of lungs, and an elementary belief in their homeland. The kindergartens vary not so much in equipment as in standards of teaching. Since the end of the war, the extremely nationalistic and even bellicose nature of some of the training has been moderated. Visitors during the war even found children learning to shoot at the age of five or six.

The compulsory primary and junior secondary schools providing universal free education to the age of fourteen have now passed out an entire generation. The entry age is now seven and at the age of eleven to twelve the children pass either into the junior secondary schools or the occupational schools. Some hundreds of thousands of pupils continue their secondary education in the secondary schools to the age of seventeen, but it should not be forgotten that by far the greater proportion of Soviet citizens complete their general education at the age of fourteen. There are, of course, many later opportunities open to them to pursue their studies in evening classes in both general and special subjects.

Soviet text-books were for many years keyed to a 'class struggle' ideology, but later Soviet patriotism set the tone, and in the past five years extreme attention has been paid to Russian national history. The Russian language and literature occupy the prime place in the curriculum which has been mainly inward-turning. World geography and world history were for many years poorly taught, though the late M. Potemkin did much to rectify this during his five years as Commissar of Education. From the compulsory schools one million boys are culled each year to pass into the occupational schools there to serve a form of industrial apprenticeship. During the war years these lads tended to constitute simply an additional source of labour; but now these scholars are receiving additional attention to their general education. In many cases the boys live communally and in a type of uniform. Over a period of years these schools have helped to solve the problem of the homeless children (besprizornye).

Much has been written of the Soviet senior secondary schools and universities. It was in the former in the early years of the Union that much experimentation took place. Though this gave way to an established type of school, there is every reason to believe that the gap between the senior secondary schools and technical colleges on the one hand, and the primary schools on the other, is as pronounced as in Western countries. From these senior schools and colleges come the hundreds of thousands who are needed as 'lieutenants and majors' in industry and agriculture. It may be assumed from the tone of Soviet pedagogical literature in the past two years that recent changes and any others which may occur in higher education will have as their aim the creation of 'whole personalities', capable of executive leadership. There are two permanent gains in the present Soviet higher educational system. These are: the broadening of the basis of the leading groups, since knowledge is open to all classes if they are capable, and secondly the rooting out of racialism. One new problem has been created by the war. The determined teaching to Soviet youth of a theoretical internationalism—which had little knowledge to support it other than the reading of selected foreign texts—suffered a severe set-back from the war. The slogan, 'Workers of all lands unite', had a hollow ring when the German army of 'workers and peasants' was camped in Russia's fields followed by armies of Rumanian, Hungarian, Finnish, and Italian pillagers. To solve this problem would require an act of faith. And faith is not willed; it occurs.

Opportunities for adult education have been organized in Russia partly by the trade unions and also by the Party. Classes in all subjects are arranged by factories and institutes and workers are encouraged to join them. Much has been achieved, especially in technical subjects, but tiredness, lack of privacy for home study and to a decreasing extent shortages of books, cause a considerable 'wastage'. Those workers, however, who have distinguished themselves as Stakhanovites or brigadiers, are especially encouraged to study. This stratum sometimes produces new factory directors; but the skilled worker does not in practice always possess a sufficiently theoretical mind to be able to train on.

In the higher schools and universities, the tendency in recent years has been to raise the standards in all branches of learning. The introduction of payment for higher education was connected with this development; as also the limiting of scholarships and stipends only to the exceptional. Before the war already forty per cent of students were children of the professional classes. For twenty years the emphasis in the universities has been on the practical sciences, e.g. engineering, medicine, geology. The need for men and women in these professions made them a 'priority'. The war, with all its deep probing into the resources of the State, and with all its brutalities, brought to many Russians a new realization of the whole value of Man. Consequently, there is at present a desire to broaden the basis of higher education, and to prevent too narrow a specialization. The humanities have received new respect. Greek and Latin are no longer pariahs, while history has been able more easily to range for fact rather than for confirmation of theory. The foreign language institutes of the universities have flourished in recent years, partly to enable the daughters of the better-paid to escape the Labour Front. In these institutes the tendency towards higher standards had already in 1919–40 led to the dismissal of a number of American radicals become Soviet citizens, whose accents in English were not considered sufficiently 'standard' for them to continue as teachers.

As the Party has certainly not abdicated, however, Soviet education is still essentially pragmatic. The philosophy accompanying it is dialectical materialism or 'diamat' as the students say. The psychology which is taught in the universities is practical. It eschews, however, any delving into the metaphysical, and at the same time rejects the work of Freud as based on an artificially narrow and inaccurate hypothesis. The actual instruction of dialectical materialism, and the cognate studies in Lenin-Stalinism are earnest and strenuous, as they are obligatory subjects. Nowadays these subjects are regarded by some students as a 'chore', the natural tendency of all students being to prefer a large meal of discussion to a dose of dogma. Thus it would be unwise to infer from the evidence so far available that the mental experience of the war years has caused the Soviet authorities to re-enthrone pure learning or pure science in the universities. Much research is being done, as before, and clearly not all of it is immediately applicable: but the general body of teaching remains firmly rooted on the ground and has a real rather than conceptual purpose.

In education, the old emotional fervour of the Revolutionary days still smoulders. The 'return of the classes' is an event each year. The reopening of the schools never passes without its ceremonies, its admonitions from leading members of the Government, its editorials concerning the quality of the young Soviet citizens who are renewing their studies. Complete issues are devoted to the event by the *Uchitelskaya Gazeta* (Teacher's Gazette). Education is firmly linked with the second aspect of maintenance of the Soviet State, which is: the instruction and exhortation contained in the press and all other media of publicity. It is only a slight exaggeration to say that everything that is printed in Russia has its aim, everything spoken publicly has been ruminated, and every poster and advertisement impregnated with social purpose.

Within the bounds of the Soviet Union there is a vast quantity of varied life. The Press which deals with it is consequently varied. But the variation is one of subject rather than of ideas or views. To a Soviet citizen sufficiently well placed to be able to subscribe to the ten or so Moscow daily papers, there would be almost as much variety of interest to be gained from them as an educated English reader can obtain from the range of London popular dailies. Moreover, Russians are accustomed to reading and understanding their own newspapers. Censorship was a highly developed instrument in Russia even before the Crimean war, one might say even at the time of Pushkin. In this book it would be impossible to go in detail into what Russian understands by the use of the printed word. Enough to say that observably the Russian is expert in reading between the lines. If the operative sentence of a *Pravda* editorial lies hidden in the second column, it will not escape the average Russian reader. He is also a great reader; he still reads for instruction. He is roughly at the same stage as the Englishman of the 1870's, at the time of 'penny-readings', before reading for diversion only had crept in.

Topical instruction is provided not only by the principal Moscow dailies, *Izvestiya* and *Pravda*, with their circulations of several millions each, but also by hundreds of provincial papers. The national and foreign news which they carry is cut to a single pattern, though there is considerable variation in the local news. Few modern devices of make-up are used, the press being throughout, serious in appearance, and the writing is stereotyped. Exceptions are the make-up of *Komsomolskaya Pravda*, the organ of the Young Communists, and *Vechernaya Moskva*, the Moscow evening paper, and the style of certain feature articles of *Izvestiya*, *Pravda*, or *Krasnaya Svezda*, e.g. an occasional neat sketch by Lidin or one of the quieter, less turbid pieces of Zaslavski. The illustrated weekly papers of Leningrad and Moscow are probably closer to those of the outside world than any other section of the Soviet Press; though they carry far more verse than a British or American editor could use. The capital also sports a weekly humorous paper *Crocodile*, which has a large sale. Like those of *Punch* its jokes are mainly social, and lack vulgarity. The paper was not at its best in war-time when it was chiefly concerned with 'blue-nosed Fritzes', but has now returned to humour about shops and flats and puts salt into jests about generals' wives.

Quantities of more serious periodicals pour from the presses—the monthly *Bolshevik*, magazine of the Party; *Literature and Art; World Economy; Under the Banner of Marxism*, etc. Careful reading of these publications does provide many a sure clue to forthcoming shifts and changes in the official line concerning politics, economics, and the arts. But the reading has to be thorough and pursuant, and is most profitable if done with a Russian's scent for the truth between the lines. For the Party member, regular 'Notes for the Propagandist' are published in large editions giving guiding-lines and talking-points on internal and international topics. In all these publications, since the end of the war, the trend has been away from the straight historical nationalism of the past four years towards the traditional themes of the Soviet Communist Party. At the same time, by the periodical and topical press, the public has been schooled to understand that the level of living can be raised only by a further spell of hard work and a vast effort of capital reconstruction.

Moral mobilization of the public has been the fundamental purpose of the Press for many years. Soviet intellectuals will admit all the monotony of what they term 'Hurrah-hurrah' journalism; but will insist also that it has produced results in harnessing the enthusiasm of the young to certain definite aims—the principal being that of driving the Russian

troika across several centuries in the matter of one
generation. The direction of this moral mobilization
lies vested in the press and propaganda section of
the Central Committee of the Communist Party.
This in turn is linked with the Kremlin Press Bureau.
The practical director is the chief Party theoretician
Alexandrov, who is a close confidant of Stalin himself. Ancillary to the Sovnarkom and thus close to
the Kremlin is also the sole news agency 'Tass',
which receives the news of the world's principal
agencies and is also provided with a staff of correspondents abroad. 'Tass' transmits Soviet news to
the outside world for reception by the Hellschreiber
system. It communicates news inside the Union by
the same system and by a series of dictation-speed
broadcasts. In this way the editorial of *Pravda* or
Izvestiya can be carried on the same day in the local
paper of Khabarovsk or Tashkent. Since normally
only the fourth page of any Soviet paper is devoted
to foreign news, not a large number of items can be
carried. The service of such news within the Union
is, therefore, highly selective. Important speeches
of foreign leaders are often published in detail but
rarely in full.

For the many who either have no access to a daily
paper or do not make the effort to read, the radio
broadcasts the news on the streets. In factories and
cantonments there are wall newspapers; and during
the war the 'Tass' Agency resurrecting a feature of
the Revolutionary days produced large numbers of
lino-cut posters, done simply and with crude effect
in bright colours.

The cause of maintenance of the system is also
served by meetings and readings in factories,

collectives, and clubs. Such gatherings usually have a specific purpose such as the voting of a resolution or a decision to subscribe collectively to a loan. To the people of other countries, such meetings may seem difficult to understand and the speeches abounding in slogans and local clichés might seem even more extraordinary. But the average Russian likes meetings and welcomes an opportunity to speak. He will utter conventional phrases with far greater eloquence than his education might suggest. Panic before an audience is rare even in the Soviet adolescent. He is one of a race which has produced an extremely large vocabulary. His language has been the medium of Pushkin and Shchedrin, of Gogol and Mayakovski and many millions of copies of their works have flowed on to the Soviet market during the past twenty years. Of foreign authors in translation, the Soviet Russian has had easy access to Dickens, Marx, Jack London, Shakespeare, Theodore Dreiser and the poems of Byron, Oscar Wilde, Goethe, Heine, Victor Hugo, etc. Kipling had a vogue in the Red Army during the war, and his positive, corpuscular mind is perhaps nearer to that of the average modern Russian than that of Bernard Shaw.

Short novels with paper covers and a serious moral tone are carried in a million pockets. Shakespeare is read in Uzbekistan. The total volume of reading is enormous. It is swollen by the hundreds of thousands of copies of children's books, the standards of production of which have risen sharply in the past five years. Even during the worst years of war a flow was maintained ranging from the intricately playful, moral nursery-rhymes of Mayakovski to luxurious illustrated collections of fairy-stories such as *Lebedi-Gusi*.

The editions of the Russian classics, of children's books, and of Soviet playwrights and poets come from the presses in editions of many thousands. Pushkin in Turki competes with Gorki in Armenian or Sholokhov in Tartar. A popular modern writer such as was the late Alexei Tolstoi need not worry at any moment about the size of his banking account. He can purchase an old painting and know that the thirst for reading of the newly literate Chuvash will still provide him with a healthy balance. Similarly the book-shops are full of 'popular educators' and the writers of semi-technical text-books can count on mammoth editions. An edition of the stylistic poet Pasternak, on the other hand, runs into a few thousands only, in company with those of some of the younger lyric poets.

Although much is written and printed, almost all that appears fits into an educational pattern. This is not only because the Government wills it, but also because the appetite of the public is serious—as serious as that of England when Macaulay was a best-seller, when Mill, Cobbett, and Bentham were studied and Dickens had passed out of the middle-class magazine serials to become fireside reading in the editions of the poor. Party literature, technical works, classics chiefly of the romantic style, and the Socialist realism of the modern Soviet writer—these form the immense bulk of the Union's reading. All contribute in their way to the maintenance of the Soviet State.

The brilliant intellectuals who cast in their lot with the Bolsheviks before or at the time of the

Revolution are gone. The experimentalism of Blok, Mayakovski, and Yesenin is gone. The phase of 'proletarian art' is long since gone; the dialectical distinction of Bukharin and Radek departed from the service of the State. What is now written covers a wide field. Especially it delves into the history and folklore of some sixty races. But its principal task is to assist in the education and the development of Soviet citizens. This era of conventionalism—since education and development demand convention—was probably inevitable at a certain date after the upheaval of the Revolution. Speaking in terms of art the atmosphere to-day is that of late Napoleon I. The new crisis of the recent war has brought a certain innovation in some of the published material and the arts, but on a small scale. Lyric, always the first sign of spring, begins to peep above the ground—sporadic, it is true, but of real emotion and quite distinct from the equally real and successful sentiment of Konstantin Simonov.

Not only is the principal common feature of all types of Soviet publicity a social purpose, but in addition they are linked usually with moral purpose. I make this statement in the same way that one would declare that Calvin worked with moral purpose. Of course, whether rules of conduct in the schools, a code of etiquette for the armed services, and a persistent education in social purpose are adequate for the maintenance of a large society is an arguable question. The Christian documents prescribe faith, hope, and charity as the necessary virtues—and the general standard of society must be set by the honesty, kindliness, and modesty of the average citizen. Observably, for some years past the Soviet Government has been prepared to allow or to favour propaganda aiming at inculcating in the citizen personal probity and stability. The chief concern of the Communist Party is avowedly with the raising of living standards, reduction of over-crowding, with State care for the individual and the creation of stable homes. The Government, however, has also given a *non obstat* to the Church. Or churches —since the Mohammedans of Central Asia are even allowed to send pilgrims to Mecca.

It is still far too early to estimate what part the Church will play in the 'Soviet way of life'. All that can reasonably be stated is what has occurred. Stalin has recognized the restoration of the Moscow Patriarchate and the reinstitution of the Holy Synod and established a mechanism by which the Synod can maintain liaison with the State authorities. But there has not in fact been any large-scale 'return to religion' in Russia. The restoration of the Patriarchate and other material signs of toleration of the Church by the State have simply made it easier for believers to attend Church. The believers are mainly elderly, but a number of young people, perhaps twenty per cent of the total congregations, also attend. The Church which has been 'recognized' once more, has emerged impoverished and short of staff. The 'Pravoslavnaya Tserkov' has, however, come through unbroken—and the 'New' Church which broke away from the Old Church chiefly on the issue of eligibility of married clergy for the episcopate, and was favoured by the authorities in the early days of the régime, has now made its submission. But the Orthodox Church which has emerged has shed many of the pretensions of the past

and its clergy will need to concentrate on their
pastoral mission as was emphasized by the late
Patriarch Sergius in his first Archiepiscopal letter
following the German onslaught.

The position of the Church in the villages has been
weakened by the State's acquisition of many of its
buildings. Those churches which remained open
before the war were heavily taxed, but despite this
the clergy were frequently guardians of considerable
funds donated by the faithful. Unable to obtain
releases of paint and materials for the upkeep of their
buildings, they had to invest in furniture and works
of art. Inside the Russian family, religion has most
often been preserved through the 'babushka'
(grandmother). It was she who prevailed upon the
young people to visit the country quietly and have
their marriage solemnized in Church, or to take the
baby for baptism. In the meantime adversity has
to some extent changed the tone of the Orthodox
Church. The people have tended to forget their
traditional attitudes to the 'pop' and his family—
according to which the priest's wife was a drab, the
daughter an unmarried mother, and one of his sons
a simpleton saint. During the war, the 'pop' often
showed himself to be a counsellor with some hold
over his community; and in most cases he supported
Russia and the Soviet partisans. The new priests
will come from new seminaries. Up to the age of
eighteen they must follow the education of the State.
After that they may study a religious curriculum in
which pastoralism is prominent.

The tact and the quality of the old surviving
episcopate was evident from the moment that the
Soviet Government allowed the Holy Synod to meet.

Since then the first contacts with the sister Orthodox Churches, the respectful relations established with the Patriarchate of 'Tsaregrad' (Istanbul), the exchange of visits with the Anglican Church—all have been managed with tact. The Patriarchate of Moscow is certain to have considerable influence in future in the lands of the Orthodox Churches; and to play its part in keeping with the new consciousness of the Soviet Union as a world power.

So far there has been no attempt to explain publicly the apparent dissonance between the creed of the Church, the essential transcendentalism of the Orthodox, and the dialectical materialism of the Party. *Izvestiya*, the organ of the Government, simply printed on its front page the 1945 Easter Pastoral of the Patriarch Alexii. In it the Patriarch admonished the faithful for failing to observe certain of their religious duties such as fasting, and reception of the Sacrament of Holy Communion. In the plans for restoration of the devastated western regions there is provision for rebuilding many wrecked churches. Materials are being set aside for the purpose. And it is significant that representatives of the Church stood on the Red Square side by side with the Government to watch the Russian Victory Parade in the summer of 1945.

The problem of philosophies is unresolved so far. For once in the Soviet Union practice has preceded theory—or rather a long gap has occurred and it is still not clear what part the Church is to play. What is certain is that the leaders of Soviet Russia are cogitating the problem of the 'whole personality', and of the 'dusha' (soul) which held the last few yards of Stalingrad. For nearly thirty years the Soviet

Union has been sustained and maintained by the opportunity of overcoming her own backwardness, and by the exhortations of a great educational apparatus. Ploughing her own furrow as she does, Russia has also to maintain herself on her own virtues. Her people have a habit of producing 'natural' saints, as another example of the extreme in their character. As for her present leaders, they have had to struggle too long and too sternly to be able to take a rosy view of human nature. But it may be that they recognize the Russians as a deeply religious people—in the proper and not the pietistic sense of the word. The new citizen whom they are forming is still immature: but the conditioning which he receives is thorough and painstaking, and the historical fact is that the system has been maintained.

CHAPTER XI
THE REWARDS

IN a society which by a definition is classless, yet is
economically in a state of rapid transition, incentive
can be maintained only by some system of rewards.
Only in an ideal world or an ant-heap will all labour
to the best of their ability merely for the sake of the
community as a whole. In Russia where the sense
of community is by nature more developed than in
many another country, there is also a temperamental
desire for lavishness, for the opportunity to squander.
In the Soviet Union this opportunity is not yet
generally afforded by the socialized stock of goods
—and in consequence there have to be great varieties
of personal reward. There is of course a fund of
general rewards; some of which had been indicated
in the chapter, 'Distribution and Consumption'.

The rewards of the Soviet way of life are indis-
putably varied. An answer is provided to the
question, 'What does a man get out of it?' Whether
these rewards are sufficiently general, or in themselves of sufficient value, to make the way of life
worth while; and whether in any case the way of
life may not be too hard for the gain received—these
again are matters of opinion. The judgment will
ultimately be supplied by the Russians themselves,
since man always adjusts himself finally to his needs.
Man as the theologians insist has a limited free-will.
However, the present facts are that the Russian, the
Uzbek, and the other millions can win higher or
lower wages, positions and privileges, decorations,

180

prizes, holidays; and take part in a wide range of common recreations. Golf and polo are open to none, and I know of no large private yachts. Otherwise all the usual pleasures of humanity are available to the Soviet citizen who can win them. You may back your fancy on the Tote at the trotting races; or if you have earned sufficient money you may arrange your collection of fourteenth-century ikons in your private dacha, or summer-house.

Soviet rewards are inevitably varied, since they are admittedly related to services rendered. From the political prisoner who earns a fuller ration for harder work done, to the People's Minister able to travel by a special coach, the gradation of rewards is long and involved. The All-Union average monthly wage in 1940 was a little over 300 roubles. But a melter in the steel industry was able to earn his 2,000 roubles on piece-work without a great deal of overtime. At present the melter probably earns something nearer 3,000 roubles. The point is that the melter is a skilled worker in a vital industry in which a high proportion of the employees have gained the title of Stakhanovites. The director of a factory may earn five or six thousand roubles monthly and that without perquisites. A book-keeper in a provincial store will earn perhaps 350 roubles and to better herself would have to move into a different type of work or a more important undertaking. A domestic servant, who is supposed to belong to her trade union, earns about 150 to 200 roubles and her keep. The range therefore of the monetary scale is of the order of one to between thirty and forty. There are, of course, exceptions in both directions. Sholokhov's banking account would be enormous did he not subscribe largely to Government loans. On a smaller scale the same is true of the joint-accounts of some peasants' families, who benefited more than most from the inflated war-time value of market-garden produce.

The State, in general, fixes payment according to services, but in the upper reaches of the scale the system acknowledges the 'surplus-value' of work done. Just as the State is anxious that individual undertakings should make profit—mainly by increasing labour productivity and cutting overall costs—and use the 'surplus-value' of their work for further capital investment, so private persons of exceptional usefulness are allowed to acquire a 'surplus-value'. This additional reward or profit which cannot be used to purchase any of the means of production, is normally taken in the form of privileges. It can, however, take the form of money or both privileges and money.

There are wide variations even in this recognition of surplus-value. Thus the distinguished scientist who is a Party member is more likely than a non-Party man to be able to advance his claims to decorations or other privileges. The writer or artist working for royalties or special commissions may earn fabulous sums in roubles, but beyond a certain figure they are of little or no value to him. Once he has a flat, furniture to his taste, a dacha, a car, sufficient clothes, and food for himself and his guests, there is little more that he can acquire. Certain groups, such as the persons connected with the ballet, have a joint surplus-value, and the members of the ballet in all the large cities are not only well paid, but also take their surplus-value in access to clothes, food, flats, etc. A member of the Soviet High Command cannot easily increase the monetary reward which goes with his position, but his position and decorations will give him access to a dacha, a car, and among other things, better education for his children. The yearly awards of Stalin prizes, ranging from 50,000 to 200,000 roubles, provide a number of persons with a usable private capital. Much of this is usually invested in State Loan, but the residue may be easily large enough for the building and equipping of a dacha. These prizes may go to Kapitsa for work on nuclear physics, or to the inventor of an electrolytic process for the manufacture of champagne, or to the designer of a new textile machine.

There have been a number of attempts to estimate how the average of Soviet rewards can be related to standards of well-being in other countries. One of the most detailed is probably that of Professor Prokopovicz, member of the Liberal Revolutionary Government of early 1917, now in exile. Prokopovicz goes into great detail to prove that the purchasing power of Soviet monetary rewards has been steadily declining, despite the increased overall production of the Union, but his view is a view from outside, based on statistics, and put forward at a time when the Soviet economy has only half completed a lengthy transitional process. A far simpler, but also factual estimate was that made by the delegation of British steel workers who visited Russia in 1945. Their reaction was favourable, not as regards the average standard achieved, but as regards the rate of progress. Both Professor Prokopovicz and the British steel workers aim at an objective view-point.

G

It is open to question, however, whether any such attempt can profitably be made. By the standards they set both Prokopovicz and the British trades unionists are no doubt correct. But one may ask whether the standards at which the Russians themselves aim will ever be those taken by foreign observers, whatever might be the social form, the economy, and the political administration of Russia? For example, will the Russian's little electric stove of to-day, mass-produced to 'utility standards', ever be developed into the table-toaster and the electric kettle of present-day American design? Russian wishes may not run in those directions.

In other words, is the satisfaction of the peasant girl on acquiring her first 'permanent' to be equated with that of the young English woman, or with that of the American girl on first wearing a grown-up Easter bonnet? In making an examination of the Soviet way of life it is not necessary to attempt an absolute answer. *Per contra*, it is necessary to bear in mind that causes for satisfaction, or the subjective values of similar rewards may vary greatly from one people to another. 'X' kopeks or 'Y' pence may buy 200 grammes of bread. But bread may be a staple food in one country and not in the other. The bread in one country may be of whole wheat and well baked, and in the other over-bleached and acidic. Low prices for classical literature may delight the young woman of one country and be a matter of indifference to the well-dressed woman of another. In the same vein, I remember a Soviet official making a chauffeur take twenty runs with a 'Zis' car at a steep snow-covered hill, in his desperate anxiety to demonstrate that the car was of sufficient power for

the job. In fact the Western onlookers were quite
satisfied that any car with or without chains would
have skidded on that hill. They were prepared to
take for granted, in complete tolerance, what the
Soviet official refused to accept. At the expense of
weakened batteries, the car finally made the ascent
in a series of skilful curves—to the immense
satisfaction of the official and the onlookers.
But the satisfactions varied. For the foreigners
present it was as though a horse had won a race.
For the official it was a national victory. Thus
it is easy frequently for the observer to regard as
secondary what to a Soviet citizen may be a great
reward.

In examining the system of Soviet rewards it is
also desirable to distinguish between personal incentives and general incentives. It is necessary further
to remember that with the Russians the latter or
general incentives are likely to be more compelling,
more effective, than in many other countries. In the
Soviet Union of to-day it is generally held that one
of the rewards of the community is a rising level of
culture. The travelled Soviet representative abroad
may admit to one that it is essential to raise this level
by a great measure and as quickly as possible. But
inside the country one chiefly has the feeling that
there is among the people a sense of development.
'Culture' is taken by them as a wide expression. It
applies as well to clean methods of eating and to
manners in trams as to the production of sculpture
for an agricultural exhibition. The newness of so
much that the Soviet millions have learned has
tended to make them over-serious as a nation—not
only regarding their work, but also regarding the

'culture' which is one of their general rewards. On these matters they display, especially in their dealings with foreigners, a punctilio and a fear of ridicule which it is difficult for the Englishman as a natural amateur to understand. The pride of the young Russian in the possession of Pushkin and Gogol is equalled by the consciousness of the other nationalities of the Union that they have their own individual cultures, which they can and do develop as a communal reward. The poet Rustavelli, in stone, looks down on the streets of Tiflis, and in Samarkand the tomb of Tamerlane has a curator. In the years immediately before the war decennial festivals of the arts of the various nationalities were held in Moscow. That of the Tajiks took place in the spring of 1941. Honoured Artists of that Central Asiatic Republic were watched by Stalin as they sang and danced in the Bolshoi Theatre. Audiences, largely of Great Russians, stood in the aisles after the performance and clamoured for more.

Art, music, and entertainment in general form a communal reward. It is true that their themes are usually linked with the single social purpose of the Soviet State. They have a revivalist flavour, since even the historical themes are chosen with an eye to the current propaganda line of the Party. But technically a high standard of performance is set. The observably keen interest of the public in music, in the ballet, in art exhibitions, in symphony concerts, is a proof that these activities are valued as communal rewards. The Red Army colonel will obtain his theatre ticket more easily than a factory girl, who may have to wait long weeks before her name comes towards the top of the list in her

factory. But both form part, finally, of an enthusiastic and critical audience. In all provincial towns
of any size the theatre flourishes. Ostrovski's *Les* is
played in Archangel, Chekhov's *The Three Sisters* in
Saratov, and the National Ukrainian Theatre performs in Odessa. Armenia staged a Shakespeare
festival in 1944. In Moscow there is an institute for
the training of circus performers and music-hall
artists, who are sent out in companies to tour the
Union. The clowns whom I saw at Saratov equalled
those of London or Paris.

Entertainment of various kinds, such as concerts,
exhibitions, and fair booths, can be seen in many
parks. These latter differ in appearance and in intent
from the Englishman's idea of a park, which is not
a falsification so much as a tidy version of nature.
The Soviet park with its statuary, its exhibition
architecture, and its slogans, purports to supply the
citizen with an opportunity for rest and culture, and
is another form of communal reward. Exhibitions,
such as that devoted to agriculture, which was open
in Moscow for several years before the war, give the
Soviet citizen an opportunity to see a chronicle of
the best of his achievements. In a land of acute
under-consumption this is in fact a popular form of
communal reward. In addition, there are a large
number of other Soviet activities which can be
regarded as general rewards. Sport is controlled by
an All-Union Committee dependant from the Council
of Ministers, but this Committee operates to a large
extent indirectly, e.g. through factories which have
their own sports' groups, or organizations, such as
the militia, who maintain football teams, rowing
crews, boxing clubs, etc. In a population with such

a large percentage of young people as that of the Soviet Union, sport inevitably plays an important role. Standards were comparatively low shortly after the Revolution, and the predominantly peasant population had no tradition of team sports—unless folk-dancing can be so termed. A heavy State investment over twenty years in grounds, buildings, and equipment has enabled a much greater volume of sporting activities of all types; and consequently the emergence of champions in each game who can rank high in international grading. Lack of international competition has meant that the best Soviet performers or players in a whole range of sports have achieved records which are slightly below the world's best. A number of world records are, however, held by Soviet Russia—one or two for trotting horses, one for swimming, and three or four for weight-lifting. Foreign observers have not had sufficient opportunity for watching Soviet rowing, diving, and tennis to be able to make a fair estimate of their standards. The Soviet Union would, however, probably have no difficulty in putting forward 'world's best' teams for gymnastics, chess, and rifle-shooting, and teams of international standard for football, swimming, basket-ball, athletics, and winter sports. In no sport are there purely professional players, although there are professional trainers. However, the best footballers are usually able to find employment in the factories which maintain the best teams, and the Government organization which maintains the best swimming-pools will be glad to give work to a champion swimmer.

Soviet sport does not differ greatly from sport in other countries, and there are few ideological tendencies, except perhaps in athletics and winter sports. As an extreme case I once watched a mile race for men wearing gas-masks and a similar one of half a mile for women; both rather terrifying examples of Slav enthusiasm. Before 1941 the Red Army had worked out an elaborate system of standards in ski-ing, and in fact the whole nation had become ski-conscious. Young children were sliding on every small slope, sometimes with only one ski.

These outdoor interests have not detracted from the Russian's pursuit of chess. His remarkable average skill in this game is perhaps also to be put to the length of the local winter. The Soviet Union is the only country in the world in which a chess tournament will pack a large hall with breathless spectators following each move on electric wall-boards or on their own cheap pocket-sets.

Ballroom dancing has begun to oust the old national dances of the Union. Not in the country-side, of course, but in the towns, where modern dance music goes always under the name of 'jazz', and the band which plays it is a 'jazz'. In the early years of the régime, when Moscow was as egalitarian as the Paris of 1791, it was customary for any man without offence to approach any woman and ask her to be his partner, but now it is more usual to ask first the permission of her male companions. This, I have been told by Russians, does not reflect any change of notion, but is simply in keeping with the general trend towards social conventions and a decorum which the world acknowledges as useful.

Two other forms of general reward exist, one rather narrower than the other. These are firstly, the activities of Osoaviakhim: and secondly, holidays. Osoaviakhim, the civilian defence organization, may seem a curious institution to set beside holidays. It did, however, provide a large number of citizens in peace-time with specialized recreational facilities, particularly at week-ends, which were a complete break from the worker's ordinary calling. Osoaviakhim was a voluntary body, through whose aid one could go camping in a para-military manner, or learn parachute-jumping (a favourite with many Soviet women), or win prizes for shooting, or obtain an air-pilot's certificate at an aero-club, complete with lounges, restaurants, etc. This organization was, of course, State-aided, as are most other Soviet recreations. Some recreations are managed by the trade unions, but they in turn are State-aided.

Since holidays with pay are the general rule (and additional wages in lieu of holidays may be claimed under Soviet law), some millions of people have in the past twenty years taken trips in summer. The number of rest-homes and holiday centres is inadequate. Opportunities to visit such places on the Black Sea coast, in the Caucasus, or the Urals foothills have had to be allotted to brigade-leaders, tired Stakhanovites and Party members, on a rationed basis. The tradition in Russia always was that one should go into the country or right back to the village during the summer; and even in the changing conditions of to-day a large number of Soviet women and children have found this still possible. The great rivers have also taken hundreds of thousands of other ordinary holiday-makers. For a fixed sum it is possible to spend a complete fortnight's rest travelling on the Moskva and the Volga, up the Kama and back. In Central Asia the Irtysh and other rivers are turned to the same use. In the south much capital has been invested in the rest-homes of the Crimean Riviera, of Sochi and the spas of the Caucasus, and the Batum coast. Soviet architects using local materials and styles adapted to the climate have here done much of their best work. The factory worker may have to wait a long time for an opportunity of visiting one of these resorts; but he has been cared for in the matter of holidays as well as could be in a country where the accent has been on the building of new cities, blast furnaces, and sugar factories rather than on rest.

These general rewards are such as appeal to the Russians, gregarious, friendly, communally patient. Insufficient they must be in a land which has created over a hundred new provincial cities—overcrowded, muddy centres, still struggling towards the individuality which constitutes a city, flowering in pathetic emotion towards the beauty of the visiting ballet, and in themselves still essentially 'provintsialnye'.

Personal rewards of various kinds were gradually introduced as a stabilizing factor to supply the incentive necessary to the executives, the managers, the Party organizers, the Stakhanovites, the Commissars, and the officers. As they are the outcome of the stabilization of a régime, Soviet personal rewards tend to be conventionalized. That is to say, the rewards which a Russian can win, though many in number, fall into a pattern. They can be utilized only inside the Soviet way of life, e.g. wages, decorations, prizes. The system of rewards has become more complicated in recent years, but no Soviet citizen has built a 'folly', or has been able to abandon the successful management of an artel to establish a large store of his own. A Soviet marshal will have his batman, his car, and easy access to the smaller luxuries of food, drink, and tobacco. But he cannot acquire an estate in the Crimea or spend six months on a cruise in the Mediterranean in a private yacht. Thus the personal rewards, though by now most varied, are rather permissive satisfactions than entirely individual gains. In the process of stabilization certain conventional forms have emerged, such as the right of the peasant to sell his private produce. Similarly, the factory director has acquired the right to his own dining-room and the use of a car—both as necessary adjuncts to his function rather than as privileges. Leading ranks of the armed services have their own clubs, as well as access to general army clubs, because theirs is a profession with special social interests, just as artists, art-workers, and the police have special interests and their own clubs.

As with any society, so in Russia higher salaries give rewards which cannot be expressed in terms only of goods bought. The local journalist who is also a correspondent of Tass and perhaps contributes an occasional article to one or other of the larger papers will not only be able to earn his 1,500 to 2,000 roubles a month. With his savings he will be able to buy an additional room or even a small flat. With a better range of clothes and a more comfortable home he will have the sense of comparative well-being which such amenities bring. He will invite local Party members, musicians, members of the professions. His life and acquaintances will be much more varied and interesting to himself than that of a factory girl. On the other hand, his work will of its nature be more open to criticism, and moving in a wider circle he will have to be more careful of his utterances. This example, chosen at random, indicates the value of personal rewards in the Soviet Union more clearly than a table of wage-scales.

Decorations further bring not only distinction in themselves but also many tangible rewards. A Hero of Socialist Labour will by definition lead an exacting life, e.g. as a prominent scientist, but he will certainly be given a flat, he will use a car, he will have sufficient money from his salary, from royalties on patented processes, from bonuses, etc., to build a dacha and to pay for the higher education of his children. He can die with the knowledge that his family can inherit his goods. The supreme authorities of the State will probably vote to his widow and his other dependants pensions usually sufficient to maintain them in the manner to which they are accustomed—or at least to give them the opportunity of working once more towards such a state. Many, in addition, are the minor privileges of being an 'order-bearer'. The values of the different decorations being more tangible are more discussed than, for example, the grades of the orders of knighthood in England. The Gold Star and the Title of the Hero of the Soviet Union are sufficient to 'make a man for life' —literally so, since they carry pension rights. But, of course, a hero is expected to continue being a hero, and the type of feat for which the order is given (such as long-distance flying record or ramming an enemy plane) is automatically dangerous. The Order of Lenin is usually given for prominent work for the State or Party over a long period. The Orders of the

Red Star and the Red Banner go more frequently to factory directors, Red Army officers, and members of the learned professions.

During the war more than 3,000,000 decorations and distinctions were awarded, and a range of new awards was created for the purpose, since it was necessary to avoid cheapening those which already existed. Some of these decorations, such as the various grades of the Order of the Fatherland War can no longer be won. The coveted Orders of Kutuzov, Suvorov, and Alexandr Nevski open in some cases only to higher officers, can presumably be won in future should war again occur. The Victory Order, with its Star of many diamonds, was by definition open only to those who planned and successfully administered operations having a direct bearing on the final victory. But the basis of all these decorations is—in addition to personal reward —the maintenance of incentive. As a Russian once said to me, 'It is not important that Major Ivanov sees in *Pravda* that he has won the Red Star; but that Colonel Grigoryev looks through the list and cannot find his name'.

The 'glittering prizes' of the régime have been instituted for a sufficient length of time to have become conventions. They now carry a certain measure of security. But the higher the post and the brighter the reward, the greater the personal responsibility. In general, Soviet privileges still go with responsibilities. There are certain exceptions, such as the favoured treatment of the ballet, the leading jazz-band directors, and the principal artists of stage and screen. In the majority of trades and callings many who have gained distinction and travelled a distance, fall by the wayside because they cannot provide all the results required from their position.

For the Soviet-born citizen of average intelligence who is aware only of the system in which he has been reared and educated, it can be said that there lies before him a wide range of opportunities and a wide range of rewards. His earnings and those of his wife, since she will need to work, will normally provide him with a somewhat monotonous supply of food of good quality, inadequate but warm housing, new clothes at infrequent intervals, and a growing supply of household equipment of medium soundness and design. Little luxuries he will also obtain with the family income; because being Russian he will make certain of them from time to time, come what may. He will get his bottle of wine, she will get her 'permanent', they will have their vodka party and play poker or pinochle rather wildly. Earlier, he would jump from job to job, but in recent years he has not been able to do so. If he lives in a large city and feels that he values privacy more than luxuries, he can on an average wage put by sufficient money in three or four years to obtain a larger room. In Moscow before the war he would have had to pay (illegally but amicably) from 1,000 to 1,200 roubles for each additional square metre. By further saving he would be able to purchase a small plot of non-arable land in the country and erect a small dacha, which might range from a hut to a cottage according to his income. In all these details I assume that he is a small workman or official with no desire to enter into public life and its attendant anxieties. His desire to have a foot in the country as opposed to a 'pied à terre' is especially Russian. The Russian is not typically a maker of gardens; but he yearns from time to time to feel country air in his lungs.

Since 1943 the Soviet Government has embarked on a programme of building many smaller houses with two or three family-flats in each structure. Thus the young Soviet couple of the future may well be able to acquire as a personal reward a useful basis for a 'stable home'. The programme will take years, but the authorities have entered on it with some determination, and a variety of designs are now being erected. If in the years of peace there is to be less of the gay movement from one trade to another, which was for long a characteristic of the Soviet labour market, then such homes may enhance the ordinary citizen's personal reward.

The excitements of new professions, of mapping, exploring, and tapping the resources of Russia and Siberia may have given an emotional experience of great satisfaction to a young people. But in examining the aspect of personal reward in the Soviet way of life it is necessary to take the evidence of Soviet figures, of the day-to-day reports of *Pravda*, *Izvestiya*, etc. We must then record that the average wage does not give a great personal reward—by Russian standards and not by the attempted translation into other standards, which obscures many accounts of the Soviet Union. For acquiring new skills and responding *pro bene* to 'socialist emulation' the factory worker does not yet gain a rich flow of agricultural produce. For changing the basis of his farming and branching into new types of crop the collective farmer does not yet gain a host of manufactured articles. Hence the creation of the system

of incentive rewards described above, and the
declaration in the latest five-year-plan that by 1950
the overall average wage shall be 50 per cent above
that of 1940.

The diplomats' uniforms and the factory director's
car have led to suggestions that Soviet Russia was
reverting to a society of classes. Privilege exists.
But such comment takes no account of the effervescent character of the Soviet scene, of its shifting
personnel and the absence of entrenched property
upon which a separate class could obtain foothold.
The honours and privileges are so far held only as a
result of constant exertion. For the mass of little
citizens the way to a full life lies rather in adding to
their own wages by making a large use of the general
rewards of the system, e.g. by joining sport clubs,
libraries, by trade union work, by visiting the parks.
The peasant, become collective farmer, may have
difficulty in buying new saucepans for his wife; but
his young children get a reasonable midday meal at
the village nursery school.

CHAPTER XII
DEVELOPMENT AND CONTINUITY

NEARLY thirty years have passed since the Galician line was crumbling in spite of the incredible endurance of the Russian soldier; since the arrest of the Tsar; since the capture of the Winter Palace and the Kerensky Government; since the cauldron months of 1917. Boys who were then aged fifteen are now Soviet marshals. Lenin has been dead and embalmed for more than twenty years. For nearly thirty years the main pattern of the Soviet régime has been unchanged. If we were to take British and French parallels we should have to write that the victory of the Parliamentarians has not led to the 'rule of the major-generals': and that the First Consul has not become an Emperor with a large and convenient family who can be placed on subordinate thrones.

True, the Comintern has been dissolved. The task of world revolution has been left to other Communist Parties with more time to spare from building sewers and minding machines. But within the Soviet Union even the most exacting war has produced no fundamental change in the régime. Various minor shifts of nomenclature—such as 'Ministers' instead of 'People's Commissars'—are merely consolidations of a long period of change. Perhaps the most important structural movement was the disbandment of the political commissars in the Red Army at the time of the struggle for Stalingrad in 1942. Even this amendment of the actual régime had been carried out once earlier for a short period, and was now being put into force again in a more definite form. Otherwise no seismic shaking has occurred; and the second General Elections under the Stalin Constitution have taken place in the same manner as in 1937, with a joint list of Party and non-Party candidates.

The Soviet way of life has, of course, not necessarily been 'vindicated' by the war of the Eastern Front from 1941 to 1945. Rather, it has endured. It has not crumbled and not changed. Perhaps the greatest mistake made by Hitler and his fellows was that of misjudging the coherence of the Soviet and Russian régime. Their assumption was that the Soviet State would fall to pieces under attack; thus they failed to recognize that over many years the Communist authorities had been constantly preaching the 'danger from without'. The centralism and the 'vigilance' of the régime had been explained in those terms. The test of the régime came and is past. Whatever modifications the visible future may bring, in the system and in the Russian way of life, will be changes of degree, within the existing framework.

There is little permanence in human affairs; but it is clear that we have to assume that the Russians and the millions of Northern Asia will continue to live a Soviet Socialist life. The one-party system continues; while the house of Soviet construction is under-pinned with beams resting on the foundations of Russia's past. Stalin in his 'Final Victory' Order of the Day assured his compatriots that members of the older generation had waited forty years to see the day of Japanese surrender and the avenging of Port Arthur. On the other hand, even in the tense days of 1942 and 1943, Stalin deliberately included in his

speeches—thought out word by word as they are—
tributes to the system of Soviets and the Party as
the storm anchors of the State. On several occasions
since, Kalinin, the former President, Molotov, and
Marshal Antonov have laid emphasis on the 'Socialist'
nature of the State. In distinction to the inspired
nationalism of the war period, amounting almost to
xenophobia, recent articles and speeches have contained hints of a recrudescence of 'Leninism'. Outside Russia it would be difficult to convey briefly
what is the significance of this word, except to
indicate that one of the factors involved would be a
return to the spirit of innovation.

In the various descriptions which have been given
outside Russia of the 'Soviet way of life', one
tendency has been to write as if the citizen has an
established and fixed existence. In fact what strikes
an observer is that for the individual citizen life has
not been static or even metric within nearly thirty
years. From the surging, starving, wander-years of
the Civil War to the era of 'thousand-per-centers',
life for the Russian has been a flow of vicissitudes.
He has known the long shudder of the Purge, when
Terror finally began to devour itself; he has lived the
years of rediscovery of Pushkin and Ivan the Dread.
During the war he has seen the migration eastwards
of some thirty millions of Ukrainians, White
Russians, etc., and a forest of chimney-stacks rising
bare from the snow over the burned villages, and
corpses stinking in their thousands in the long pits
outside Kharkov and Odessa.

The normally well-read person of Western Europe
is familiar with many of these changes; from the
early experiments in integral Communism in some

villages, to the education decrees of 1943 and the present reconstruction of the Dniepr Dam. In Central Asia the former nomad now knows that he is a member of a collective farm, growing tea, and that the tractor clatters beside the immemorial camel. During a quarter of a century of incessant change, patterns of industry and social conventions have, however, crystallized only slowly. And now a war has delayed the process; a war which devastated regions producing nearly half the crops and the coal of the Union. One of the principal achievements of the first year after the return of these territories was the provision of temporary housing for two and a half of the millions of people whose homes had been destroyed and who had been forced into a stroglodyte existence in holes in the earth.

The history of Russia is of a series of frustrations within and disasters from without. But in the present case the significant fact is that although much was destroyed by the recent war, nevertheless much was also developed, especially in the thousands of square miles east of the Volga and of the Urals. On this occasion, as was so often not the case in Russia's history, the crisis is past without a breach in the leadership, and the economy will continue to be planned. Down in the villages they have seen the winters through on potatoes and millet only—as they have done during wars in the past. But this time the Slavs have emerged from the ordeal preserving the trappings of a modern industrialized State. Across the regions formerly occupied lay the moral sludge left by the German tide, but much of this will by now have been shovelled away and the Soviet pattern of order and exhortation re-established. Within the

State boundaries, somewhat enlarged, the Fourth
Five-Year-Plan, covering the whole Soviet Union,
has been put into operation. The size of the Plan is
in itself an indication of the size of Russia's needs,
and at the same time of the extent of Russia's
unusual victory.

After a dissection of the main aspects of the Soviet
system it is perhaps possible to attempt a consideration of Soviet life as a whole and its impact upon the
individual citizen without hazarding an *ex cathedra*
judgment. It might be said that in a subjective
manner this is what educated Russians themselves
have been attempting to do since they were sub-
mitted to the detailed examination of a war. The
early elections and apart from them a vast amount
of discussion have been the principal features of the
Soviet post-war scene. A volume of discussion has
always been going on inside the Soviet boundaries,
since the Russian is an inveterate talker. Sometimes
the discussion has been mainly behind closed doors;
at other times it has swollen into a chorus of self-
criticism, denunciation of bureaucracy, or enthusiastic promises of greater production. Now the Red
Army man has returned self-conscious in his victory,
confident, more experienced in life, cunning with a
soldier's cunning, to face life again inside a system
which of its nature is governed by an army of
officials. As I have mentioned earlier this is an army
of Russian officials with Russian traits inherited from
the days of Tsarist bureaucracy. The demobilized
soldier resumes his job in a land of the internal passport, and of much 'paperasserie'. Since there are a
hundred public jokes on the subject, and since such
things are the standby of the Soviet music-hall

artist, it is essential in any consideration of the Soviet citizen's life to mention the 'spravka', the general paper of entitlement, the document which enables one to go a journey, to obtain new car tyres, to obtain petrol coupons. To gain a 'spravka' it may be necessary to make a 'zayavleniye', or declaration, backed by an 'otnosheniye' or substantiation from some recognized body. If these documents bear a square rubber stamp they may rank as evidence; if they have a small round stamp they will carry weight; if a large round stamp they will have effect—and with an additional small diamond-shaped stamp to indicate that they have not only been issued but also verified, they will command an attention which it would be unwise to withhold.

Nevertheless a generation has grown up within this system, is now largely literate, and though of varying competence itself is able to recognize incompetence. This generation knows how to move about within the system and understands what are its legitimate short-cuts. This generation uses glibly all the accepted contractions of Soviet terminology. Words which are still contractions in the minds of the older generation, such as Sovnarkom, Glavlit, Mogiz, etc., have become part of their language. In another few years many of these words will have merged entirely into the great Russian vocabulary. Most of them are not beautiful, as was the residue which remained in the French tongue from the experimentation of the Pleïade. But they are autochthonous; and most of that which is distinctive in the Soviet way of life and endures will be autochthonous.

The children on the streets, after a war of privations are lively and fresh-cheeked, not only because the State has paid attention to them, but also because the Russian as a human being likes children. The Russian is also capable of great endurance, and the Government capable of an ice-cold display of will-power. Thus many elderly people faded and died during the war, from tiredness and under-nourishment resulting from the smallness of 'dependants' rations. The elderly in any case are aware of other systems, and remember another Russia—one of greater ease of manner and of mental ease also, one in which failure could be tolerated with a warm-hearted cynicism. It is on the elderly that the war has worn heavily. But the young and the old both provided heroes of the resistance in the occupied regions. They were Russians in a Fatherland War. On the other hand, most of the Volga Germans were shifted eastwards *en masse*, and after the German retreat from the north Caucasus a large proportion of certain local races, such as the Cherkessy and the Ingushy were moved into Kazakhstan. Nevertheless the war crisis has passed without another period of general purge: Stalin having promised in early 1989 that the era of political surgery had gone and would not come again. Already in Siberia some of those people of brilliant attainments who were sentenced or deported in the stark days of 1936–7 are working in semi-liberty as school-teachers, doctors, etc. Once more they are being used in the opening up of Siberia. Of the Union as a whole, what is not yet discernible is whether the atmosphere in these post-war years will revert at once to the sense of achievement which was apparent in 1940–41.

To some extent this must be so, not only because the war has been won, but also because there has been no break in many spheres of production. In spite of all the difficulties, of all the illogical enthusiasms which planning tries to overcome; in spite of the battered appearance of the motor-car, which often seems to be held together by one wire, the machine progresses. Katya, my Soviet maid, once remarked to me regarding the peasants, whom she, as a city dweller, looked upon quite objectively, 'Nowadays they have their printed dresses and their shoes even if they do not work in them.' The factory director and the railway official have become technically more efficient in the past twenty years. Girls have become traffic police, and as the Soviet tradition is to treat women on a level footing with men, they are normally able to direct without argument.

On the other hand, the main energies of the nation have been put into the use of new tools, new factories, the building of new buildings—and all Russian towns could now do with a new coat of paint, more plumbing repairs and more maintenance generally. In the same way that the streets are cleared of snow from one day to another in some towns by volunteer working-parties, so perhaps one day a fiat will be uttered and the whole nation will bustle and refurbish their own home. Such a sudden effort would be in line with their nature. Meanwhile the villages are emerging from 'behind the forest', though the war undoubtedly slowed this process. The villages are real and dirty and alive again after their numbed uncertainty of the early 'thirties.

The Russian is more aware of the mood of his community than are the people of most other

nations, and even within the Soviet planned way of
life mood counts for much. The mood of the past
year has been to make use of whatever aid the State
or any other agency may bring towards individual
recovery and the regaining of the sense of achievement which was rudely shaken in 1941. From a
country with so many young people this is expectable;
but what is genuinely Slav about the former sense of
achievement is that even in the midst of personal
discomfort they were proud of what they had made.
As opposed to this very real national consciousness
of worth there were certain aspects of the Soviet
scene which could be ranked as façade or 'Potemkin
villages' after the favourite of the Empress Catherine,
who erected painted settlements of cloth and batten-
ing on the banks of the Volga when his ruler made
a ceremonial voyage down the river. To a foreign
observer such 'villages' are the exhibition statuary
to be found in many a city and park, the resounding
mathematics of percentages, the involved articles
explaining the rightness of previous decisions.

The Soviet system was applied, roughly speaking,
by a working class—and in its development there
was an inevitable lag until that class had begun to
supply persons qualified to design or to invent with a
high standard of skill. It is an observable fact that
inside Russia the new way of life—whether efficiently
or inefficiently—did provide the opportunity. The
naïve inexperience from which the mass of Russian
workers and peasants started in 1917 simply adds
a lustre to all that they managed to achieve, and
deepens the shadows of all that they have suffered.
As ever in Russia values tend to be absolute; to be as
white as the snow or as black as the pines.

On the evidence available conditions of life for the Soviet citizen are likely to be just as mobile in the next twenty years as in the past. Perhaps the voices in the wind of the steppe will be less immanent, less urgent. But the prerequisites for a static Soviet life do not yet exist. The next twenty years must automatically show drastic change, even were development to proceed at no greater rate than that of the 1930's. The reconstruction era on which Russia has now embarked is not the same, however, as that which began in 1921. At that time production in industry as a whole had fallen to a fifth of what it had been in 1913, and the total agricultural production had fallen by a half. During the past war, on the contrary, it is certain that overall industrial production had by the end suffered no catastrophic fall, while in some of the heavy industries (steel, chemicals, etc.) there was undoubtedly an increase. Similarly, although agriculture was seriously hit by the first two years of war, it was already past the nadir when the last gun was fired. The effect, then, of the first world war and the Revolutionary period was qualitative; that of the past war has been by contrast quantitative. Reconstruction this time will take place in a Soviet Union of many new features— one of small house planning, of rules of courtesy for schoolchildren, of medals for prolific mothers of sober character, and of mobilization of scientific brain-power upon problems of electronics and nuclear physics. It will take place in a nation of which the dialectical centre of gravity has moved eastwards. The new factories of the Urals, of Karaganda and Tashkent, will not be stilled, but will give birth to other heavy and light industries. Millions of those

now living in Asia will never die in the Ukraine and
White Russia from which they came in the tumult
of 1941–2. If we accept the population of Siberia,
Kazakhstan, and the Central Asiatic Republics in
1939 as 59,000,000, then, taking into account the
effect of the recent influx upon the annual total of
births, we may reckon that these territories will,
before the end of the century, house no less than
100,000,000.

The development of economic regionalism, which
was a feature of the interrupted Third Five-Year-
Plan will be resumed. In particular, the economies
of the Soviet Far East and of western Siberia will be
brought to equilibrium on larger total budgets. The
relatively neglected Soviet navy is also due, according to Stalin himself, to be considerably expanded.
The Fourth Five-Year-Plan already in operation
confirms that the fundaments of Soviet economy are
being maintained on lines sketched in an important
article published in *Under the Banner of Marxism*
towards the end of 1943. This article insisted on
the necessity for the deliberate erection of laws
in socialist economy, on the need for reduction of
industrial overall costs, and further increases in
labour efficiency. Individual enterprises must make
a reasonable profit so as to assist the investment
financing of the Soviet Union as a whole. A socialist
theory of surplus-value was to be the inevitable
concomitant of continuous economic expansion.

The nation already launched on the new capital
plan is young in its average age, and younger still
in the willingness of its members to marvel or to
feel awe. Before the time-worn Sphinx they would
exclaim with simple enthusiasm. As against this

youngness it has to be taken into account that the whole nation has in one way or another put out an immense effort for some thirty years. Many of its people must be ineffably weary. This strain comes nearest to expression in the words of an important Soviet citizen who said to me, 'We *must* raise the level of our people's life—and quickly'. Addressing a gathering of peasants in the November of 1945, ex-President Kalinin admitted that some of the returning Red Army men had been impressed by the creature comforts of German life. He asked them to reflect that a spiritual bankruptcy lay behind this material façade, compared with which the Soviet way of life, he declared, was both more moral and more varied. From the evidence available it seems that a large number of the Soviet soldiers who have had contact with the Balkans and Central Europe have, on the other hand, been relieved rather to return once more to their own soil. Historically the Ukrainians and the Russians have preferred their own lands, their own atmosphere and their own ways, with which the Soviet system for all its ideological basis is impregnate.

In October 1945 *Izvestiya* carried two items on the same day, typical of the Soviet way of life which this book has examined. One was a short report, 'Est li khozyain v Gryazestve?', which may be roughly translated as, 'Who is in charge at Gryazestvo?' A short and sharp denunciation of lack of effort. The second was an article detailing the history of the Kremlin Cathedrals, the spires of which were at that time being relieved of their war-time camouflage paint. At the same time, one learns, the students of the universities were discussing, as still they will,

'What is the meaning of democracy?', 'What is personality?', 'Why the Big Three?' and, 'What are the responsibilities of the Soviet Union as a Great Power?'

Ten years only had passed since the Constitution was being discussed throughout the Union, and a war had brought them back close to the cold fundamentals of life, to the 'bone within the skin'. And in the relief of victory they were arguing out their horizons as students do. Meanwhile the weekly *Crocodile* had introduced a section of foreign humour; an import which a tested and undefeated Soviet Union could afford. At home its fun was directed against the eccentricities of generals' wives. Hence, an examination of the Soviet way of life at this moment reveals it as a contradictory thing, as questing and striving and as established and conventional.

INDEX

For Product Safety Concerns and Information please contact our EU
representative GPSR@taylorandfrancis.com
Taylor & Francis Verlag GmbH, Kaufingerstraße 24, 80331 München, Germany